Pra
"Hanging on for Dear Life

"In my 45 years of medical practice I was never involved with a more incredible case, the amazing outcome of which was greatly influenced by Jim's determination and grit, and the tremendous loving support of Beverly."

Dr. Ben J. Birdwell, MD, Internal Medicine
Summit Medical Associates, Hermitage, TN

"Beverly has put into words, in a powerful way, human expressions of the victory and the defeat of a family dealing with this horrific disease. "Hanging on for Dear Life" is for anyone who is searching to learn how to live through cancer and even become stronger because of it."

Sue Z. McGray, Mary Kay Independent
National Sales Director Emeritus,
Author of "Becoming Visible", Old Hickory, TN

"Beverly and Jim have been on a long journey together, fighting his cancer. This story will share the insights they have gained along the way. Their faith in God has been put through fire as they have battled this disease numerous times. The result has been a faith that has seen them through the darkest days and rejoices with them in the care of a loving God. I believe this book will give encouragement to others who are traveling a similar path. Their love is inspiring and their faith gives hope."

Susan Boyd Beasley, Library and Information Science
Metro Nashville Public Schools, Nashville, TN

"With her faith, wit, and wisdom, Beverly Fetzer Oakley shares firsthand the story of many years of emotional, physical, and spiritual ups and downs while she and her beloved Jim hang on for dear life.

Their story holds great encouragement and inspiration for all who read it."

Kim Yarbrough DeHart, Sponsor, William Harold Yarbrough
Room at the *House of Compassion*,
Rochester church of Christ, Rochester, MN

"Beverly understands first-hand the unexpected twists and turns that life can take. You will be blessed as she shares how her faith has kept her uplifted and encouraged through this journey she and Jim have traveled. God continues to use her as an encouragement to others."

Barbara Bennett, Counseling Ministry Assistant
Gulf Beach Baptist Church, Panama City Beach, FL

"'Hanging On For Dear Life!' What power and accuracy! If you or someone you love has ever had the dreaded diagnosis of cancer that is exactly how you feel. Beverly is the very essence of a southern lady. She says out loud all the things that the rest of us thought and wanted to say, but didn't, and she does it with humor and candor. As you read, you will laugh and you will cry. You will be a better person and friend to others from having gained this priceless insight into the life of a cancer patient and his wife, caregiver and love of a lifetime."

Linda Kidwell Bell, Lone Star College, minister's wife
Houston, TX

"Although the Lord sent Jim and Beverly down a path they would never have chosen, they have embraced this life with prayer and love, leaning on family and friends. Beverly shares how God has led them through this disease and how they have found blessings through adversity!"

Beverly Wright Atwood, Teacher, Goodpasture Christian School
and minister's wife, Nashville, TN

"If you or someone you know is going through a life-changing illness and you don't know how you're going to make it through another day,

I highly recommend this book! Beverly recounts the 31-year journey of her husband's cancer with tremendous realism, passion, wit, and eloquence. You will laugh and cry as you walk through the battle with them. One thing is certain: all who read it will be blessed!"

Debbie Johnson Davis, Mary Kay Independent Consultant
Old Hickory, TN

"If you are in need of guidance for the many questions of dealing with your own cancer or the cancer of others, please read this book."

Dr. Wes Carnahan, PharmD, BCPS, Clinical Pharmacy Specialist
Tennessee Valley Healthcare, Nashville, TN

"Most of us are fairly confident we will eventually meet God, but we're hoping it will be many years from now... at the end of our lives... once we have gotten ourselves all sorted out and are somehow *ready* to meet Him. Obviously, that's not how it works. During the past three decades since my Uncle Jim was diagnosed with cancer, our family has met God again and again. He suddenly shows up in our lives amidst nightmarish news, prayerful pleading and miraculous moments. We have all ridden life's rollercoaster, alternately white-knuckling the safety bar in desperation and prayer, then throwing our hands in the air explosively as God thrills and surprises us, leaving us all-at-once grateful, exhausted and exhilarated. We have loved doctors and Christian servants whom we have never met for blessings we never expected, and we have learned that when we ask for the Holy Spirit to work among us, He shows up with Power and Verve! I stand with the whole Oakley family as a living witness to the incredible story of Jim Oakley as he (we) have been Hanging On For Dear Life...and what a *Dear Life* it is!!!"

Gavin Gossett, Branch Manager Residential Finance; Director,
JAM Films, Woodmont Hills church of Christ, Nashville, TN

Hanging On for Dear Life

Our Family's Victory over Cancer

Beverly Fetzer Oakley

BEVERLY FETZER OAKLEY

WESTBOW
PRESS

A DIVISION OF THOMAS NELSON

Copyright © 2013 Beverly Fetzer Oakley.

All rights reserved. No part of this book may be used or reproduced by
any means, graphic, electronic, or mechanical, including photocopying,
recording, taping or by any information storage retrieval system
without the written permission of the publisher except in the case
of brief quotations embodied in critical articles and reviews.

THE HOLY BIBLE, NEW INTERNATIONAL VERSION®, NIV® Copyright © 1973, 1978,
1984, 2011 by Biblica, Inc.™ Used by permission. All rights reserved worldwide.

WestBow Press books may be ordered through booksellers or by contacting:

WestBow Press
A Division of Thomas Nelson
1663 Liberty Drive
Bloomington, IN 47403
www.westbowpress.com
1 (866) 928-1240

Because of the dynamic nature of the Internet, any web addresses or
links contained in this book may have changed since publication and
may no longer be valid. The views expressed in this work are solely those
of the author and do not necessarily reflect the views of the publisher,
and the publisher hereby disclaims any responsibility for them.

Any people depicted in stock imagery provided by Thinkstock are models,
and such images are being used for illustrative purposes only.
Certain stock imagery © Thinkstock.

ISBN: 978-1-4908-0969-4 (sc)
ISBN: 978-1-4908-0968-7 (hc)
ISBN: 978-1-4908-0970-0 (e)

Library of Congress Control Number: 2013917390

Printed in the United States of America.

WestBow Press rev. date: 10/02/2013

Table of Contents

Dedication

For Jim:
You captured my heart such a long time ago and hold it still today. Should we live to be one hundred years old; even then, it will not have been enough time together.

Introduction

In 1982 when my husband Jim was diagnosed with a rare chest tumor, to say we were blindsided would be an understatement. We were in our thirties with two young children. He worked at Ford Glass Plant. I was a new Sales Director with Mary Kay Cosmetics. We were active in our church and I taught Sunday school. We enjoyed family vacations to Disney World, the mountains, and the beach. Fishing was also a family favorite; our son and daughter loved to water-ski and boat ride. We couldn't have asked for a better life.

We were told the tumor was malignant, extremely aggressive, and difficult to treat. He was given three to six months to live. Our doctors in Nashville diagnosed the malignant thymoma, but due to the rarity of this tumor, treatment here in Nashville was not an option. We were directed to M.D. Anderson Cancer Center in Houston, Texas. We left our children with friends and family, and the next chapter of our lives began. Our new life in Texas consisted of medical tests, waiting for results of those tests, and hoping for a cure. In the midst of all this my strength came from prayer, but my coping came from writing.

This is not a story about me; I'm just the writer. I present views from the standpoint of a caregiver, wife, mother, grandmother and occasionally a frustrated woman. I lived it. So did a lot of other people. Those who were present during the making of our story will have their own interpretation of how the story went. My purpose in sharing it is to help others who are dealing with cancer or other life-threatening illnesses. I want to lend some helpful tips on visiting people with chronic illnesses, and to demonstrate how to be a patient's advocate. I also hope to communicate how- through unwavering faith in the Almighty God and by supplication to Him- we will be given the strength we need to cope. Even in the midst of our doubt, He will always answer us. He will supply every need and will fight for us when we cannot do it alone.

"Is anyone among you in trouble? Let them pray. Is anyone happy? Let them sing songs of praise. Is anyone among you sick? Let them call the elders of the church to pray over them and anoint them with oil in the name of the Lord. And the prayer offered in faith will make the sick person well; the Lord will raise them up. If they have sinned, they will be forgiven. Therefore confess your sins to each other and pray for each other so that you may be healed. The prayer of a righteous person is powerful and effective."

James 5:13-16, NIV

CHAPTER 1

In Sickness and in Health

It was March of 1982. I knew something wasn't right with my husband Jim. He didn't feel well. He had a hoarseness that didn't go away. He was plagued with frequent upper respiratory infections. He was fatigued most of the time. He had an irritating dry cough. A thirty-six year old man shouldn't be feeling this way. He had regular check ups, but nothing was found to be abnormal. He went to all the right doctors for the symptoms he had. They would treat him, but soon he'd be sick again. I had never in our sixteen years of marriage seen him have persistent health problems. Most symptoms would go away with rest or a dose or two of some over the counter medication. I knew something was wrong.

By April he began to experience a nagging pain around the top of his right shoulder. It gravitated to his lower right side and to his back. The pain continued to worsen. I rubbed his back with one of those potions for sore muscles and gave him a mild pain reliever. We hoped that by administering these medications, combined with rest, the pain would be gone. Despite my efforts, the pain persisted and moved to his right lower chest. He developed a low fever and had a tingling sensation in his right hand. I suggested we go to the emergency room. He was agitated and irritable. My suggestion wasn't well received. He said he would be fine and I should drop this whole thing.

I decided to make a little deal with him. I told him I'd call a nurse at the emergency room and talk with her about his symptoms. If the nurse said they were nothing to worry about, then I would drop it and leave him alone. He finally agreed to that. I called the nearest hospital. Of course a nurse isn't going to wave off your symptoms. I knew she was going to advise us to check them out if we felt there was a problem. Finally, he relented and reluctantly agreed to go to the ER.

It was storming fiercely that night, and if I hadn't been so insistent on his being seen immediately, we would have chosen another time. I was nearly frantic with concern. He was feeling worse with each day. I knew he wouldn't take a day off work to go to the doctor. This was the only way I knew to have a doctor see him.

At this point, I must tell you Jim's words to me: "I don't need to go to the ER. There is nothing wrong with me. I have just pulled a muscle in my right side. When you take me to the hospital, they will say you are crazy and will admit *you* to the mental ward!"

He had been helping some friends do a roofing job the week before, and that job probably helped to save his life. He had carried several heavy bundles of roofing material up the ladder. He expected some muscular discomfort, but not pain that didn't subside. The pain he was having may have been muscular, but the fact it didn't subside with use of a mild pain reliever caused us to seek medical attention. It didn't seem right for pain from overworked muscle discomfort to worsen.

At the hospital emergency room, they did a chest x-ray, and the doctor said the results showed something suspicious in the area of his right lung. He thought perhaps it was scar tissue from an old case of pneumonia, but in order to be sure it was nothing more, it was suggested he be admitted for further tests. As we were getting Jim settled in his room, no one mentioned my needing to be seen by a psychiatrist that night, or ever again.

By morning, Dr. Ben Birdwell had seen the results of the x-rays. He discussed with us the possibility of this being some type of respiratory infection or the result of scar tissue but he had no definite diagnosis. He didn't want to dismiss Jim until they had a firm diagnosis. He said he would call in Dr. Michael Minch, a thoracic surgeon. Further tests were ordered and executed, none of which gave us any firm answers...yet.

Jim was given a course of antibiotics, yet the symptoms persisted. He was given a stronger pain pill. It was at this point I was certain we were up against something bigger and scarier than anything we'd ever faced in our lives. Both lungs were functioning normally, and his pain was being managed. He was discharged from the hospital. We would come back later for further tests, allowing him to go home for the weekend and rest, continuing the antibiotics. Our doctors were concerned, as were we, as to what was causing this pain. There were still unidentified spots in his chest. They had not cleared with antibiotics.

On April 11, a sample of fluid was drawn off one of the spots on his right lung. Several diseases were ruled out. It wasn't tuberculosis or histoplasmosis. I knew his case was being discussed with several oncologists in Nashville. I supposed that cancer cells had been detected and they were trying to find the type. I was hearing of a lot of concerned chatter suggesting we put him in another hospital. Our friends and family worried about our neighborhood hospital's ability to handle Jim's serious health issues. They wondered if he should be at one of the larger facilities. I knew our doctors were doing everything humanly possible to make a firm diagnosis. The hospital was not the problem. The disease they were tracking was the problem.

On April 30, Jim was dismissed from the hospital to go on a three day fishing trip with some of his buddies to Center Hill Lake. It was a good idea. He might not be able to go again. On May 3, Jim was admitted once again to Donelson Hospital for a few more tests. These would give the final diagnosis. On May 4, a frozen section was done. A piece of the tumor was resected for testing.

During the procedure, about a hundred people had gathered in the waiting room. The word of Jim's illness had been such a shock, and so many caring people were there to support us. The room was jam-packed. I escaped to the hall and waited there. The noise of all the voices was enough to make my already aching head explode. I just wanted to see the results Dr.Minch would find from the biopsy.

It was only a few minutes until he came down the hall toward me. The look on his showed serious concern. He looked right into my eyes.

"It isn't good news. I took the sample to the lab myself; I didn't want to trust anyone else's impression. Jim has a very serious disease. It could be one of several. It is malignant. The best we can hope for is some type of Hodgkin's disease or lymphoma, but what I fear is cancer of the thymus gland, a malignant thymoma. His entire right lung is involved. It is a large mass."

"Why can't you just remove it? Just get it out!" I asked in a controlled panic, searching for answers.

"It is too aggressive and just too large. He wouldn't survive if I just went in there and started taking things out. We are not equipped..." His voice trailed off.

"How long does he have then?"

"Maybe three months, six months at the most." he said, his eyes beginning to show signs of tears. No need for more words from either of us.

"Thank you. Would go in there and tell his family, please?" I pointed to the waiting room and started to walk up the hall just to see if I could do it. I was numb. I couldn't feel my feet on the floor. I could not think. My heart was in charge.

The next thing I knew, my brother in law, Sonny Gossett, was on one side of me and his mother, Nettie Rose, "Nan," Flippen, was on the other side. I really wanted to be alone, but those two knew it wasn't what I needed. I noticed a small restroom and started to go into it. I hoped to get away so I could fall apart in peace and quiet. Nan didn't see it that way. She edged right into that little restroom with me and bear hugged me as I bawled. She began to pray aloud.

"Lord, this child has just been hit with some horrible news. She is all to pieces and needs *you* to pick her up and dust her off so that she can carry on. Help her to be able to handle whatever comes along. Be with her precious family and heal her sweet husband, Jim. Make her strong, Lord. In Jesus' name, Amen." Then she handed me a wet paper towel for my face. We left the tiny restroom and were rejoined by Sonny. The three of us went outside where we walked until I could feel my feet on the ground once again.

I needed to compose myself before I went back inside. Jim would be in recovery for a while. I would be able to see him soon. I regret not going back into the waiting room during the report. I simply was not able. My reaction was hard enough. I did not want to witness the reaction of anyone else. After the doctor left, I went in just long enough to hug my children and make plans for their afternoon. I saw that they were being cared for by our good friends Carlos and Freida Denny. They took our children home with them that afternoon and cared for them most of the next few months.

They later told us that on the way home, our son Greg broke the silence.

"My mom and dad always told us to be positive. My dad will get well." Everyone agreed. The mood lightened and the group went straight to McDonald's.

That day had to be one of the toughest ones for us all. What good friends, Carlos and Freida! Kristy, our daughter, says she has no memory of those first few days. I know that she was frightened, poor baby. There was so much love and hands-on care for our two children. The fear had to be softened by all the attention they received for the next few months. Many friends and family had a hand in making sure Greg and Kristy were taken care of while we were gone.

CHAPTER 2

Putting Our Armor On

Whatever we faced was not going to snuff the life out of our family. Cancer might destroy a lung, but it would not destroy our family or our faith! After some time of dealing with my emotions, I suited up for the fight. Even though my heart pounded in my ears from time to time, I knew there were some things I must handle. I knew I wasn't alone, many prayers were being prayed.

Jim remained groggy from the biopsy. I watched him sleep for three days. He'd wake from time to time, but he wasn't coherent enough to hear the results of the biopsy. It was tough enough for him wake up from regular sleep, but with the added effects of surgical drugs, he was not waking quickly. I needed him to wake up. I needed him to be able to think clearly. I needed him to be aware of our crisis.

"I can do all things through Him who gives me strength" (Philippians 4:13, NIV) echoed in my head. I began to feel a new calm. I was beginning to learn about peace. I looked at him as he slept and dreaded telling him what was happening inside his once healthy body, yet he needed to know. I prayed myself into a state of calmness for him and for our children. I needed to focus minute by minute. There was so much to consider. I felt numb. My heart was ripped into shreds.

This monster in his chest was threatening to take away the very life of my husband, the father of our two children, the love of my life. We had only been married sixteen years. That wasn't long enough. I felt a part of me had died. I wished I could exchange places with him. On the first night in the hospital, in the early hours of the morning, a nurse came into the room to check on Jim. She told me I should sit down and try to get some sleep. The chaos in my head was keeping me awake.

"You have been standing beside his bed for hours. My shift is over, but I'd sure like to see you sitting down before I go home." She asked if I'd eaten anything, and surely I had, for there were people around who probably offered me food. I really hadn't realized I'd been standing there beside him for so long. I wanted to be sure I was the first person he saw when he awoke.

It was three days before he was able to move around, to eat and to keep his eyes open. I told him we needed to discuss the test results. We also needed to tell our children. I asked our good friends, Jim and Beverly Atwood to be with us and our children in the hospital room as we talked to them about their daddy's illness. Jim Atwood prayed a beautiful prayer for us. Jim and Beverly's presence made it easier to give our children the news. It helped to soften the harshness of reality. God's peace had wrapped its arms around us all. As the days went by, I was actually able to answer the questions the children asked. God was holding me up and giving me a kind of strength I'd only heard of. I'd never had need of such strength. I could feel the effects of the prayers on our behalf. They were working. I was feeling calm and strong.

I stayed at the hospital almost around the clock. I'd go home around five each morning, shower, and make sure the children had what they needed. I'd go back to the hospital and have breakfast with Jim. I was always able to hold my tears until I got into my car, and there, alone in the dark early hours of morning, I would drive home and cry until my head ached. I learned that tears were an important part of coping.

We had a command post set up in the lobby of the hospital. Jim didn't need everyone to come to his room, and there were other patients to consider. All during the day and early evening, people would stop by to visit with us. We made sure that one of us was there in the lobby so none of the visitors would have to leave without seeing some of us. Their support was important to us. People are good when there is a crisis; each wanting to do something to help bear the burden. I felt the effects of the burden being lightened often. I was able to spend a great deal of time with Jim. We treasured every hour, not sure when it all might change.

Somewhere during these times I was able to tell God I would not selfishly hold on to this man. This man was His, not mine. God loaned me this remarkable man, but He didn't say I could keep him. I felt a burden was lifted after I had my big grown-up talk with God. I took the children aside one night and told them if their daddy died, our life as we knew it would continue on. We'd learn to cope together. I told them we would still live in our home, have our car and all our stuff. I know children get worried about things like that. I told them we would find strength together to face each day. My children would never have to wonder where my heart was. It was of paramount importance to me to be a strong example for them. It still is.

Jim and I discussed heaven, death and other issues. He wanted to sell his boat and his Bronco. Our son was fourteen.

9

A Bronco would be a good vehicle for him in a couple of years. The boat could sit there. I wasn't willing to see any of Jim's possessions go out of the driveway unless he was driving them.

We knew Jim's prognosis was worse than bleak. This thing was an extremely rare chest tumor. It killed people. We had arrived at a point of acceptance, but didn't want to give up hope. I knew how concerned everyone was about Jim. We never felt alone during those early days. We were so thankful our good doctors made a correct diagnosis. We knew they would continue to take care of Jim.

Dr. Minch came into the room the afternoon Jim was dismissed from the hospital and we talked about options. He told us we might consider going somewhere like Sloan Kettering, Mayo, M.D. Anderson, any number of places that might help give Jim more time. We discussed the rarity of this type of cancer and how it wasn't known to respond to treatment. Yet, his demeanor and his words held promise for the future. I knew we weren't without hope. We weren't going to give up. Calm washed over us as Dr. Minch spoke. We checked out of the hospital and went home with a feeling of positive expectancy.

A few days later, we received a call from Jim's sister, Linda, who lived in Miami at the time. She and her husband, Bill, had been discussing Jim's diagnosis with a friend of theirs who was a physician. When they asked him what he would do if it were one of his family members, he said, "I'd get him to Houston to M.D. Anderson so fast it would make his head spin."

Our life was about to pick up speed. We immediately called Dr.Minch and asked him to set up our appointment at the M.D. Anderson Cancer Center in Houston, TX. He and Dr. Birdwell agreed we should go quickly. Plans were being set into motion.

So many good people assisted us in every way! Linda and Bill provided our round trip plane tickets to Houston. We were being lifted up in prayer, given gifts of money and offers of assistance to make our trip as easy as possible. We even had people to go to Houston with us! Jim had been on a lay off from his job at the Ford Glass Plant for a while. It was not the best financial time for any of the Ford Glass families who were affected by the lay off.

Our children would stay here at home, spending time with family and friends. They would be fine. We saw no reason to subject them to long hours of hospital waiting. We had no idea where we would stay or how long we would be there. It was a scary adventure, but God was in charge. We would go to the cancer center in hopes of buying some more time. And yet, there was an outside chance nothing could be done for him. In that case, the clock was ticking, three to six months to live, spinning by much too fast.

Ronnie and Mary (Jim's brother and his wife) planned to be in Houston with us. They would drive their car from Nashville to Houston. Jim and I would fly Delta. Ronnie calculated the driving time so they would be waiting for us at the airport in Houston. When we boarded our plane in Nashville, we knew Ronnie was driving toward Texas like the wind. The fourteen hour drive would require him and Mary to drive all night. It would be more than encouraging seeing their smiling faces at the airport.

Just after we were seated, a flight attendant announced that passenger Jim Oakley should turn on his light. Jim looked at me with a puzzled expression. The flight attendant came over and quietly asked to us to follow her. We were being moved up to first class. Brother-in-law Bill Arnold had instructed the flight crew to move us if there was seating available. Captain Bill was still flying for Delta then.

Ronnie and Mary were at the airport in Houston to pick us up. Ronnie's calculations were perfect, of course. Big brother was always on time. Ronnie and Jim had their usual detailed conversation about the road trip as we drove toward the hospital. The next order of business was to find a hotel for these weary travelers.

Jim's appointment at M.D. Anderson was scheduled for the next morning. The four of us had arrived in Houston just before Memorial Day. We were not in a mood to celebrate, but we would make the most of this situation. The reason for Ronnie and Mary's driving, besides the fact Ronnie likes to drive was that we would have a car while we were here, and someone to drive us. After checking into our hotel, we drove around Houston, exploring the part of the city around the hospital. We had dinner, and then retired for much needed rest. We were up bright and early the next morning and on our way to M.D. Anderson Cancer Center for the first time. We would be seeing a surgeon.

CHAPTER 3

The Battle Begins

During Jim's first visit with the surgeon, it was once again confirmed the tumor was malignant thymoma, stage IV. We were told they would need to move quickly. We were moved to another exam room with three surgeons. They asked Jim to sit on a stool in the middle of the room. They began to turn him around as they discussed how to gain access to this monster in his chest. Their ideas all seemed like they'd leave a big mark! One mentioned going in the back, one talked of removing ribs and going into the side. Another mentioned just going for it! I could not even imagine what they were going to do to my husband. I just wanted them to make him well again. After they stopped the stool spinning, they left the room to collaborate.

One of the surgeons returned to the room to say surgery had been scheduled for the following Monday, June 2. That would be in three days!

The surgeon who would be Jim's, said,

"These tumors normally don't respond to treatment. They are hard to remove, and they most always come back. The best we can do is to get in there and see if we can de-bulk it and maybe follow up with some treatment."

We agreed and soon made our way toward the hospital's admitting office. Jim asked the doctor how many of these he'd removed.

"Ahhh, about four or five, I'd say." Jim asked him if he'd seen a lot of them. "Sure, quite a few, a lot of them." the doctor said and confidently left the room. We'd be in Houston a while.

Ronnie and Mary had been scouting out the other hotels and found a nice apartment at the Anderson Mayfair. It was just across the street from the hospital. It would be walking distance, and I would feel safe going to and from the hospital. It was a better deal, though still expensive, it suited our needs perfectly. We knew if we told Jim we were going to move, it would be a stressful decision for him. We decided we didn't need his input this time. Ronnie, Mary and I moved our belongings while Jim was getting some last minute ex-rays at the hospital. We were anxious for Jim to see our new home! Mary had set up a pot of coffee, ready to plug in, and set out four cups. As our eyes excitedly scanned the apartment, we all smiled and agreed it was perfect. We had a large living room with a sofa bed, a large bedroom with two queen beds, and a nice kitchen and bath. Both large rooms had windows over looking Astro World. We were told we could expect a spectacular fireworks display each evening as the park was closing. We could hardly wait to share all this with Jim!

When Jim finished the hospital details, we drove over to pick him up. The three of us were trying not to show our excitement. Mary and I were trying our best to keep a straight face and suppress our giggles. Jim could tell something was going on. He searched each of our faces for a clue, but found none.

Ronnie said to Jim in his most serious voice,

"We've been looking at some places to stay and we have one we want you to see." Jim asked Mary and me if we'd seen it. We told him we had. He'd no sooner asked us where the place was, until we were parking in front of it! We entered the hotel and took the elevator to the eleventh floor. We went to the door of one of the apartments, opened it and walked in. We strolled around the rooms, each of us making positive comments about it. One of us had plugged the in the coffee pot as we passed the kitchen. The aroma of coffee brewing was inviting.

Jim walked into the kitchen and said, "Hey, they've got a coffee pot like ours! It sounds like it is making coffee!"

We all laughed and the three of us said, "Welcome home! We live here now!"

He didn't argue. He just sat down and got comfortable with his freshly brewed cup of coffee. Mary and I chose those moments to take pictures, because we were all genuinely smiling. The Anderson Mayfair would be our home for a while. We enjoyed watching the fireworks every night. It was like having our own private collection of shooting stars to wish upon.

Jim was admitted to the hospital on June 1. We were still wearing our happy faces. Jim was ready to get this done! Our minister, Ron McIndoo, had flown in to be with us all during surgery. Our friends at church were providing strength for each of us by sending Ron. We had been told in Nashville the tumor was massive and Jim might not survive surgery. We knew there was a possibility I might have to fly back alone, with an empty seat or a stranger beside me. That would be a task even the strongest couldn't be asked to endure. I appreciated the fact that every detail was being handled. What loving and caring friends! It would be gratifying to have our minister there with us.

Our congregation would be happy to receive a first hand report when Ron returned. We knew how concerned and prayerful our friends were at church.

We sat with Jim the night before surgery. We had prayers and we had a few good laughs. We had come to this place for him to get well. He did not want us to sit there and stare at him. There would be plenty of time for sitting later, and for staring.

Jim wanted Ron to experience some real Texas style beef brisket while he was in Houston. Our favorite restaurant, Buck and Charlie's, served the best. Jim insisted we go. We needed to be good hosts. We would come back and see him after dinner.

We were on our way to the restaurant. Mary and I were seated in the back, riding in silence. Ronnie was driving, chewing his unlit cigar. Ron was riding along, also in silence. We knew we should eat, but no one was hungry. As we rode along, country music was playing softly on the car radio. I felt every word of the sad song wafting out. Tears began to well up in my eyes. I tapped Mary on the arm. Mary leaned forward and quietly asked Ronnie to turn off the music. It wasn't like anyone was listening to it anyway.

I could listen to screaming, wailing, hollering rock music, but not anything with heart and feeling. I was much too transparent and fragile to listen to love songs.

I knew I needed to be strong for the time ahead, and I couldn't let a mushy song bring me to tears. We arrived at the restaurant and suddenly everyone was ready for dinner. We were seated, ordered, got our chips and salsa, and were able to enter into some light conversation. We did fine. I gazed out the window at the traffic and answered when spoken to. They were kind enough to let me be quiet.

When the food arrived and I'd had my first few bites of brisket, the jukebox started up and Tammy Wynette blasted out "Stand by your man."

You've got to be kidding me. The brisket I'd just put into my mouth got bigger and bigger as I tried to chew. I was finally able to take another bite when the song was about half through. We couldn't ask them to turn off the jukebox just because I was a whiney baby. After our dinner we drove back to the hospital to visit with Jim. It would be the last time he would see Ronnie, Mary and Ron before surgery. I would go back in the morning. We visited, had prayers, then the four of us left for the Anderson Mayfair.

I was up at four a.m., trying to keep quiet as I dressed to go to the hospital. I focused on trying to look nice, because I sure didn't feel well. Tension was giving me a headache, stomach cramps, and a back ache. I also felt nauseated. Other than that, I was okay. I tip toed out while it was still dark, for the short walk over to the hospital. I felt numb, and the song playing in my head was "Stand by Your Man."

When I got to Jim's room the nurse was giving him instructions on showering with a germ-killing cleanser. She told him they would back in a few minutes to wrap him in sterile sheets. I asked her if I could kiss him after he was wrapped. She said I could. I waited while he showered, my mind going in no particular direction, yet running thoughtlessly in every direction at once.

Jim with two lungs, one kind of messed up, got out of the shower, dried off, and in came the mummy wrappers! Two nurses swooped in, unfolded a green sheet onto the bed, instructed him to lie down on it, and they turned him into a green mummy right in front of me. He was bound up like King Tut, only not as fancy. They left the room, leaving him mummy wrapped. He wondered what he would do if he needed to go to the bathroom. They came back, much too soon, to take him to the surgical area. It was easier for me to let them take a green mummy than to take my husband. They even let me kiss the mummy goodbye. I choked back tears as he was wheeled down the hall and out of my sight. I wondered if that would be the last time I saw him alive. We knew the risks.

It was still dark outside. I turned off the lights in his hospital room, and while sitting in the darkness, wondered how a small town kid from Manchester, Tennessee got into such a fix as this. I had a mini pity party for one. Nobody needed to have been there for that. I wasn't able to cry. I thought my chest would burst.

I found the surgical waiting room and found a seat, hoping this room wouldn't be filled to capacity. The surgery would begin at eight. The surgeon told me it would take three hours and if I saw him sooner than three hours I would need to be worried. He said someone would come out midway through the procedure and update me. I felt relieved having Jim in this competent surgeon's hands for the next three hours. Whether he had removed one or twenty one of these tumors, I didn't care. This tumor today was the only one I cared about.

Ronnie, Mary and Ron joined me in the waiting room. Jim's brother Charles and his wife Elsie were visiting family in Houston and were able to come sit with us during surgery. While we waited a nurse came out a couple of times, giving updates to let us know all was going well. The waiting was tough. The good reports helped ease our minds.

In exactly three hours, the surgeon came out of the double doors, his expression hopeful and positive. We sprung out of our seats and circled him. He looked right into my eyes and said, "I cannot tell you how massive this thing was, but we removed it. We also removed his right lung and every bit of tumor we could see. We scraped his chest cavity until we reached healthy pink tissue. He is stapled together inside his right chest wall. He will be in surgical intensive care and will have his own nurse beside him. We are not totally out of danger. There is still a possibility he could hemorrhage. The next twelve hours will be crucial and you won't be able to see him. Go home and rest. It is ok for you to call as often as you want, but go for now go home and sleep. He will need you later."

We thanked him, he hugged me and left. A nurse appeared with papers and phone numbers, and I felt sleepy for the first time in days. We all grabbed a quick bite and Ronnie took Ron to the airport. I thanked Ron for coming out to be with us. I told him I knew if things hadn't gone well in surgery; it would have been tough for me to fly home with Jim not beside me. He smiled and said, "Yeah, we wouldn't let you do that."

I went back to the apartment, and collapsed onto my bed. I never bothered to get up and change clothes. Though I did remove my shoes, I slept most of my twelve hours in a navy skirt and white blouse. Ronnie and Mary called the intensive care unit to check on Jim several times. Upon hearing that he was stable, I would continue resting. I was aware of the many phone conversations as people called to check on us, I was just unable to take part in them.

CHAPTER 4

Stand By Your Man

The next morning I showered, dressed and walked over to the hospital. I left Mary to take care of Ronnie, who was reclining on the couch twisting his hair. I felt it best I see Jim this first time by myself. I entered the surgical intensive care area and inquired about Jim. They told me I could see him for a few minutes. I was not prepared for what I would see. The nurse directed me toward a thin pale man in a bed in a glassed in area.

I didn't think it was Jim. There were machines connected to him. He had a tube the size of a vacuum cleaner hose going into his mouth. The tube was taped down, across his face, pulling his lips into a horribly uncomfortable looking angle. He was making a gurgling sound. His hands were taped to the bed rails. The nurse led me gently to his bedside. I was sure she would discover that she had brought me to the wrong room. Then I saw Jim's eyes. They were his clear sparkling blue eyes, but they were full of fear. He looked at me and tried to say something. He tried to move his hands, but they were bound to the rails. The nurse told me he had been trying to remove the breathing tube. That was why his hands were strapped down.

I looked at him again and told her, "He is frightened! Untie his hands and give him a pencil and paper."

"We tried," she said. "He can't write to make any sense."

She handed him the clipboard and a pen once again as if to show me his inability to communicate. He was flat on his back, a nurse holding a clip board, and the pen wouldn't work upside down. He was frustrated as well as frightened. I asked her to get him a pencil. He was agitated. He glared at me, the tube making a gurgling sound. She said he needed to be suctioned. He appeared to be drowning. I felt helpless. She handed him the clipboard and this time the pencil. He glared at me again and wrote as I waited to read his first words to me after surgery.

On the clipboard was scrawled: "Get Out."

He put down the clipboard. He motioned for me to leave, and once again needed to be suctioned. I patted his arm. He jerked it away and pointed to the clipboard. The nurse turned her attention to him and I left the room. I walked up the hallway and just stood for a minute. I slid down the wall and sat in a heap. I felt extremely nauseated and light headed.

I saw no reason to go back into his room at this time. It would only upset him again. He needed to be calm. I walked around for a while wondering what to do next. Suddenly it was clear to me! He thought he was on the respirator forever. He thought he was on life support. Had they not explained to him what was happening? I rushed back inside to speak to the nurse. I told her he was frightened and asked her if she would explain to him that the tube would be removed when he was able to breathe on his own. I needed her to tell him he wasn't dying and the respirator wasn't permanent. I also told her he normally had a hard time waking up. They would need to reassure him more than one time. He simply might not be awake enough to hear them. I still didn't even look into the room where he was. I wanted to see him, but I didn't want to upset him again. It was evident that my presence wouldn't help him yet. I didn't want him to be upset again today. Not by me, anyway.

I went back to the apartment and found Ronnie and Mary waiting anxiously for a report. I told them he was doing fine. I called the nurse several times during the afternoon and evening. He was still unable to breathe on his own. He was sleeping most of the time. I slept from mere mental exhaustion. My being able to rest now would renew my strength and I'd be able to care for Jim more effectively when he was moved to a hospital room.

The next morning I made my way back to the intensive care unit and was greeted by his nurse. She said he had done well during the night and they were about take him off the respirator. They had been weaning him gradually and it was time to see if he could breathe on his own. His body had to learn how to function with one lung. This meant that his heart had to adjust also. The nurse told me to go have some breakfast and come back in an hour. I decided to wait until the giant tube was out before I gave Ronnie and Mary a report. We needed some good news, and if the tube had to go back in, I didn't want to have to pick Ronnie up off the floor. I also didn't like the smell of ammonia they use when you slide down a wall and faint. Never mind how I know this.

The hour I waited finally crawled its way by. I returned to the unit to see Jim sitting up in a chair, looking better, but still pale. His breathing was a bit labored, but he was breathing with no respirator required. He had a couple of drain tubes in his chest, one in each side, a couple of IV's and a catheter. He required two poles to hold up all this apparatus. Now that he was able to sit up and was breathing on his own, I could see that he was feeling more hopeful. I walked over to him and leaned over to kiss his cheek. My hand rested on his arm. He screamed.

JIM'S SIDE OF THAT STORY

Jim's perspective on waking up in
intensive care (as told to me):

"When I woke up I couldn't tell if I was alive or not. I had a tube the size of a vacuum cleaner hose in my mouth that went nearly to my stomach. I was strangling. They would suction. They suctioned a lot, but not enough. I'd put my hand up near the tube to tell them I needed suction again. They tied my hands down. My heart was banging and clanging nearly out of my chest. Every time it banged like that, I thought it would throw me out of the bed. When I was finally able to make them understand that my heart felt like it was trying to jump out of my chest, they said it was learning to function with one lung. I thought I would be dead before it finally learned. They had been telling me the tube would come out when I could breathe on my own. All I understood was that I couldn't breathe on my own. I didn't know how long I'd been there. I knew I had been asleep but I didn't know how long. I didn't know if it was night or day. There was always a nurse beside me. All I had to do was open my eyes or move one finger and they were magically there to help me. They were trying to keep me calm. Then they would tell me to wake up. I was awake. I thought I was dying and that they had put me on life support. I figured someone would disconnect me soon. When a nurse came in and said it was time for my bath, I thought, "Why waste water? Let the undertaker bathe me." I wondered why they were bothering with me.

Then when *you* came in, you looked beautiful. I remember you were wearing a green dress. Your smile was pretty. Your eyes looked beautiful. I hated that you were seeing me looking almost dead. When I wrote *go away* I wasn't mad at you. I just wanted to spare you. I didn't want you to see me like that."

CHAPTER 5

A Long Road to Recovery

"Oh! You are hurting me!" I jerked backward, wondering what I had done to hurt him. He told me he hurt all over and not to touch him. I thought to myself,

"This is going to be a long road back." He had had enough of sitting up and motioned to the nurse to help him back into bed. He would remain in intensive care for another day and night. I continued my visit to the allotted time, mostly so I could see his progress. He didn't really care if I was there or not. Two days later, we were told he would be going to a regular hospital room. We were elated beyond words. He was now able to breathe with one lung. He had been walking several times each day. He was getting stronger.

Our support team was overwhelming. We had people in Houston and people at home. Everyone was doing what they could to make this bearable. We received many cards every day, all of them full of words of hope and encouragement. Sometimes we'd receive thirty or forty cards in a day. I had never realized the impact receiving a card could have. I promised myself I would do better at sending people cards!

I continued my uncontrollable urge to write things down, sometimes the words on the pages, along with the prayers being prayed, were the only glue holding me together. I spoke with our children daily, and most of the time after hearing their voices, retreated to some quiet place to cry. I missed them so much, and I missed our life as we had known it. This hurt. I knew people were taking care of them, but it was hard for me to be away from them.

During this first part of the hospital stay, while Ronnie and Mary were there, Mary would relieve me a couple of times a day from the hospital sitting. It gave me a break to get outside and walk around, plus the hospital was so cold that it just about froze me out. It was a good time for Jim to have a break from me too. Mary and I would keep notes on the daily progress of things. Jim's sister, Linda came from Florida to visit, and was able to sit with him in the hospital for a while. It was always good to have another helper on board. Carlos and Freida took turns taking care of our children in Nashville and taking care of us in Houston.

Jim continued to improve while he was in the private hospital room. He began to eat well and did everything the doctors told him to do. We walked the halls about three times a day, carefully guiding the two poles of necessary apparatus along with us. Soon the chest tubes were removed and replaced with small bandages. He wanted to walk more frequently since he was told walking would help him get stronger. One day, as we were walking, I asked him to slow down a little, for he was walking faster than me!

One of the things that bothered Jim most was an intense back ache. We understood this would become less of a problem as his body healed. One night he was having more pain than usual. He didn't want to ask for anything stronger for pain. We were ready for the time when pain medication would be a thing of the past. He wanted to get well. I was rubbing his back and hoping to make it better, when a beautiful nurse appeared in the doorway. She was small and dark and looked to be of Indian descent. She asked, "Is he in pain with his back?"

"Yes, he is." I told her. "Rubbing helps."

"May I show you?" She entered the room and walked over to Jim's bedside. She indicated he should lean forward. Her tiny hands began to move across his back, quickly and skillfully she pressed and rubbed as she looked over at me as if to instruct. I thought she might ask him where his back hurt, but she was touching the exact areas of pain I knew much too well. She kneaded muscles in the middle of his back, both to the right and left of his spine. She walked her swift fingers methodically up and down his spine. She ended the session with a slight smile, nodded and left the room. The name Mary was on her name badge. Later that night, I rubbed his back in the way Mary had demonstrated. He slept through the night and was ready for his walk in the morning after his bath and a hearty breakfast. When Jim's nurse came by to check on him, she asked about his back pain. We told her we'd like for Mary to come in again and give him another back treatment.

"Mary? Who? When was that?" We told her all about the beautiful lady in white with her dark skin and the little red dot in the center of her forehead. She looked more puzzled by the moment. She excused herself, saying she'd be right back. When she returned she brought another nurse with her and again we told the story of Mary. They smiled and shook their heads as we told them. They seemed slightly confused by it all. When the story was done, the second nurse said, "We are extremely security minded here, and the fact is, we don't have a Mary on this floor. We don't have anyone fitting Mary's description. I know all the staff on this floor and our volunteers work during the day."

Our nurses were trying to offer an explanation. We didn't want one. We were fine with Mary. We never saw her again. Who knows when we may be visited by angels? Angels have always existed and if God wants to use them, He can. They are His. And we are His also.

CHAPTER 6

No Place Like Home

On June 26, we were told we could go home from Houston for ten days. We had never felt such excitement and barely slept the night before leaving. We would be coming back to Houston for radiation treatments, but the thought of home was making us blissfully happy. We could have flown without a plane!

It was good the doctors allowed us to go home for a short time. It proved to be an important part of healing before radiation treatments would begin. Jim was glad to get into his old comfortable chair again. It had been difficult for him to find comfort in any position. Even with his familiar old chair, he continued to get up many times during the night to walk around. The back pain was still a problem and moving around helped ease the pain. Though the incision from surgery was healing well, quite an impressive one, he had the most discomfort from the little punctures from the drainage tubes. They were deep and would heal in time.

On the last night we were home, he slept all night without waking. His back was healing. Home just felt good. We were to be at home for ten days, but we received a call from our Houston doctors asking us to return two days early. Treatment had to begin quickly. It had been a good break. Eight days home was better than nothing. We packed our belongings again, not sure how long we would need to be in Houston for radiation, and went to the airport.

It was extremely difficult for me to leave Nashville this time. I wouldn't be home for my daughter's twelfth birthday. Plans were made and she would have a good time, I knew that. My being with Jim was more of a pressing need, yet it was painful to leave my children once again. As we boarded the plane, Jim noticed our children and a group of our friends waving to us. Jim enthusiastically waved back.

"Wave to the children!" he said. I looked and waved and felt tears welling up. I was glad they couldn't see us. He waved and I cried until they were no longer visible to us. I cried most of the way to Texas. The flight attendant noticed my apparent sadness and offered to get anything I needed to help me feel better. Jim was handling leaving much better than me. It was glad we didn't have our down times at the same time. He quietly gave the flight attendant some brief details. She smiled and brought me a package of tissues and a soft drink. Her gesture of kindness did help me to feel better.

I knew radiation was going to begin the following day. We had been told the radiation treatments wouldn't make Jim sick. We understood the side effects were minimal. We hoped that the next few months our life would be normal, except for going for treatments every day. We would be living in Houston for several months. In truth, the only normal part of that plan was that Jim and I were together. We were fortunate to have friends with us, sometimes Ronnie and Mary, sometimes Carlos and Freida. I missed the normal part of me, the mom part. I prayed

I was doing the right thing by being here instead of at home. I felt guilty and torn.

When we returned to Houston for radiation, we needed to find a more long term residence. We found the Brompton Place Apartments. It was a lovely complex only a few minutes from the hospital. There was a swimming pool just outside our back door. I spent as much time as I could beside the pool. It was a quiet place to write. Writing helped me cope. It provided a kind of therapy. I could write what I didn't need to say out loud to anyone. I didn't want to burden anyone with my recurring feelings of hopelessness.

On the morning of June 30, I wrote:

"I don't know what is going on inside Jim's body. I don't know if that monster in his chest did more damage than can ever be repaired. I don't know if he will ever be strong again. I have to be positive for him and for everyone who loves him. I get tired of being strong. I hate this. There are times when I want to scream and cry and render myself unconscious so I won't feel this pain. It hurts to see him lose weight, vomit and creep slowly from room to room. There are times I wish I'd never heard of him. I wish I'd been born another person in another place and time. Maybe then I wouldn't care. I want to tell everyone to go away. I am tired of being here. I want to go home. No words can help. I cannot handle this. No one can change this."

After I'd rail out like this, just my notebook and me, I would feel much better. My personal load became easier to bear. The pain in my chest went from a throb to a dull ache. The ache could be blotted out by a good night's sleep. I felt so small and this job seemed so big. I didn't sign up for a gig like this. Where was the happily ever after?

Life at our Brompton address was as good as we could make it. When our friends or family was there with us, we shared cooking chores as well as clean up duty. Mary and I would take a brisk walk around the complex each night after dinner. It gave us a break from our work and was good for us both physically and emotionally. When Carlos and Freida came to be with us, they took over the kitchen, cooking and clean up. Freida and I would walk after dinner. It was a blessing to have them with us. Carlos had a knack for knowing when I needed to get out of the apartment. He'd find an estate sale and would say we needed to go see what they had. I was usually working feverishly on some kind of needlework. I didn't know how to enjoy needlework. It became an obsession. I'd make something and give it away. I was ready to get it out of my sight. I would always start a new needlework project, even though my handwork projects seemed to present yet another job for me to do.

CHAPTER 7

Treatment Is No Treat

On the first day of treatment they marked an area on his right chest with a red marker that would have to stay for the entire course of treatment. He would not be able to get the area wet, meaning a shower was out of the question. I would be giving him a tub bath every day as well as washing his hair, drying him and dressing him. It wasn't an easy task. He was weak and became weaker as the treatments continued. He could not bend forward because of the huge incision from his back shoulder blade area to the front of his lower right ribcage. He always felt better after his bath and hair washing, but the process caused him pain. The bath process usually took about two hours. He would be totally exhausted afterward. His once muscular body was now emaciated. He had less of an appetite than before surgery. He was rapidly losing weight.

After the first radiation treatment, he became nauseated and coughed until he vomited. He was being given nausea medicine in pill form. He couldn't keep the medicine down. And he couldn't keep food down. It seemed to me the doctors in radiology were not hearing me when I told them how sick Jim was. They gave him injections for nausea. They were trying to help, yet I wondered if they didn't see that he was getting worse. They saw him every day. I wasn't sure what to do next, but I was sure I'd think of something. He was getting thinner and weaker as each day passed. I hurt for him. I could not see how he would live through this.

They told us radiation didn't cause nausea. We knew nausea first hand. They continued to try to find a medication that worked. One afternoon we went home with another new nausea medicine. Jim took it after treatment and it looked like it would work just fine. We were sitting in the living room relaxing after dinner. Jim suddenly began to have a horrible reaction to the medicine. His right arm began to pull outward and upward in a painfully unnatural position. I called the emergency room and told them what was happening. They agreed he needed immediate attention and for us to bring him in quickly. They said we would be faster than an ambulance. You bet we would! We have Big Ron.

Ronnie drove us to the hospital at warp speed. We rushed Jim in to see the doctor. They immediately gave him something to counteract the side effects of the compazine and he was relieved of the problem. He was fine to go back home with us, and he was without nausea meds again. They said he'd sleep and the injection they'd given him should quell the nausea. I hoped they were right about that. However, he slept fitfully and moaned a lot. I could tell he wasn't resting, but the muscle spasms never returned.

The nausea and vomiting were back with us by morning. First coughing and then the same scenario would unfold. He would begin coughing and then lose his food. He was losing alarming amounts of weight. We were not winning anything here, unless the radiation was working on the chest wall. We had it all covered with prayer, but fear still crept in from time to time.

During the night, I had an epiphany! I thought of what we'd used for nausea when the children would have virus and vomiting was one of the problems. I could ask Jim's doctor to prescribe phenegren suppositories. Nothing else was working. I didn't mind asking for a prescription, but I was afraid to ask the doctors about Jim's prognosis. I learned if you weren't given one, you probably didn't want to ask. One night I penned a wish or two:

"I so desperately want Jim to live, but only if he can be healthy. Neither of us wants him to be an invalid. I pray that God will spare his life only if he can live happily with us as a family. I know there must be some great lesson in all this. God, help me to see it. I need to lose the fear and focus on hope." I felt like he was dying right in front of me, and my desperate attempts to save him were not working. I tried to sort out the shreds of hope and not dwell on fear. The lowest times for us all were when Jim was experiencing these horrible side effects. We felt helpless.

When we went to the hospital each day for treatment, it worked best for Jim and me to be dropped off at the door. Jim wasn't able to walk from the parking lot to the hospital entrance. I would take him inside and begin the walk to the treatment area while the driver parked the car. He refused the use of a wheelchair. He would have to stop and rest several times. The driver had time to park the car, walk to the hospital entrance, and join us on the long walk down the hall toward the treatment area. It was a bit of an ordeal, but together we made it work. We couldn't have made it alone.

M.D. Anderson in 1982 had a sterile hospital look. There were shiny tile floors, loud speakers paging doctors, waiting areas with uncomfortable chairs that sat much too close to the person beside you. Televisions screamed out their noisy game shows, news reruns and soap operas. In the waiting areas, walls were lined with brochures inviting you to take one so you could learn about the type of cancer that you were battling. There were no brochures on thymoma. Thymoma was a rare and scary chest tumor no one needed to know about.

After a few radiation treatments, we met another physician, an oncologist. He and I got off to a bad start. I think I must have been sitting on his stool or something. I didn't like him and he didn't seem to like me any better. I really didn't care for his attitude. His answers to my questions made me feel like he thought I was stupid. My questions needed positive answers and he didn't have any. I finally asked him if there was something I could read concerning thymoma. He said there wasn't anything except journals with case studies in the physician's library. I told him I'd take it. He frowned and told me none of it was good, as he wrote out a visitor's pass for the physician's library... and read about the monster that was killing my soul. He was right. There was nothing good. I read case studies where people got it, fought it and died of it. I knew Jim's case would be different. Even though the librarian made copies for me to take, I decided not to read them anymore and instead focused on positive reinforcement. I folded them and put them in the back of my notebook. We were fighting an unknown enemy and it was deadly and dangerous. I now had the papers to prove it. We armed ourselves with prayer and positive thinking. We were going to win. We were not going to lose to this beast!

Another thing we did not lose was our sense of humor. Laughter was good medicine and we never missed an opportunity to have a good laugh. We were careful not to spend time with people who wanted to share stories about the people they'd known who had died with cancer. A visitor we had back in the hospital at home in Nashville left quite an impression.

It was during the first weeks of learning that Jim had cancer. A well-meaning man came by to visit us on a Friday night. We were happy to see someone come by on a Friday night. No one visits sick people on the weekend! We were somewhat bored. We welcomed him and looked forward to sitting and visiting for as long as he wanted to stay. The first few minutes went well as we caught up on what was happening in his life. Then he started up with, "I knew a guy who had what you have." The more he talked, the sicker his guy in the story became.

Jim stopped him.

"You don't know anyone with what I have." He said.

"And does this guy die at the end of this story?"

"Well, yeah, he died. He didn't make it. He died in six months!" Our visitor replied excitedly, He was totally unaware of how helpless and his story was.

"We don't need to hear about anybody who dies." Jim firmly stated. Case closed. Story over. The visitor stopped his death story, fumbled around a minute, looked at his watch, stood up, apologized for having to leave so soon and left. We thanked him for coming by to visit. As soon as he left, we just looked at each other. I admit, we did laugh a little, but not where he could hear us. We appreciated this man's visit. We did. He just wasn't aware of the absurdity of his subject matter. He was just trying to make a visit.

We have learned much over the years. We visit people from time to time when they are sick. We make it a point to visit on the weekend. We learned what not to do. We visit to encourage, to give hope and to do whatever we can to show the patient we care.

Each phase of our cancer experience helped teach us to be better in many ways. It is when we are in the valleys we learn. When we are on the mountain tops we aren't always teachable. From time to time I personally experience overwhelming moments of clarity. I hope to always have them no matter where I am in life. It is during those moments I realize that I have learned something from life. Nothing that has happened to us should be tossed away as unimportant. It is all a life learning experience.

I finally found the courage to ask one of the doctors about Jim's prognosis. The doctor was leaving the exam room. I followed him into the hall.

"Doctor, may I ask you a question?" He turned in my direction and nodded.

"Can you tell me what Jim's chances are for a normal life?" He just stood there looking at me like I had just asked for the impossible. The silence was becoming a bit uncomfortable and I wondered if he planned to answer me at all. Me. Pollyanna, looking for happy. Me. A leprechaun, come to fetch my pot of gold.

Finally he said, "He doesn't have any."

"What do you mean? That he won't live a normal life or he won't live at all?"

"Well, if you mean will he be well enough to play football, no."

He was getting ready to walk away when I said, "I don't need to talk with you any more. I don't like your negative attitude." We stood there looking at one another for a minute. I asked him if I could meet someone who had a thymoma. He stood there quietly for a moment and said softly, "No."

When I asked him why, he said, "I know of no survivors."

I couldn't say much for my mood the rest of that day. That was the day I tried to crochet. It didn't go well either. I crafted a mangy looking chain. It barely qualified as a bookmark.

Later that night I tore up the copies of the case studies and threw them in the garbage. How could I compare Jim's case with any of these? I wondered about each of them as I read them one last time before trashing them. Had they been Christians? Had people prayed for them? Did they have family who loved them? Was their home life chaotic or was it peaceful? What was their caregiver like? Did they eat well? Did they rest well? Of course none of that information was there, just the medical jargon, age at diagnosis, involvement of the disease, course of treatment, and when they died. Not good reading material, really. But I really had to know.

The next day when we went in for treatment I asked the radiologist for a prescription for a phenergren suppository. When we got back to the apartment, Jim used the suppository and slept most of the afternoon with no nausea. That evening he ate dinner and kept it down. No coughing, no nausea. I felt like we were onto something good. Jim, Ronnie and I were able to watch television and laugh. Houston life felt fine. Things were once again good, or as good as they would get for a while. I wondered why they hadn't thought of a suppository before all this, or why I hadn't thought to suggest it.

Each day when we'd go for treatment Jim would become weaker. I practically had to carry him to the door once he got out of the car. We looked like a couple in a three legged race, only much slower. We both came to dread entering the radiation area. I will never forget the smell. It was somewhere between burning flesh and chemical attempts to cover up the smell of burning flesh. The halls were forever winding and marked with a red line down the floor. It was cold, sterile, and not attractive. The chairs were uncomfortable and the waiting area was small and stuffy. We would wait and wait and wait some more. It was hard for Jim to sit very long at a time because of back pain. I'd rub his spine, which felt like bones with not much more than a tissue paper thin covering of skin. The only good part about the waiting was when it got to be our turn to see the doctor; he would give us all the time we needed. Patients were never rushed through.

Jim would finally receive his treatment, we would take him home, and he'd go to sleep. I would pray that he would live through the night. These scary parts have nothing to do with the care he was receiving at the hospital. They were doing everything humanly possible to destroy this beast. The beast is responsible for all the scary parts.

One night as we were in bed, I looked over at Jim and I could actually see his heart beating. He was so thin. At that point I put my hand on his shoulder and prayed,

"God, he is so weak and I am healthy. If it is possible, just let some of my strength flow into him. I cannot see how he can make it through this night unless you help him." I was grasping at anything to hang onto! Like I thought he could be healed through osmosis! Each night as we got into bed I'd have him visualize the cancer cells in his body. I'd have him describe them. Sometimes they'd be bright red, sometimes deep black. Then, we'd visualize Pac Man to the rescue! Pac Man was the cancer killer, and we'd say, "Chomp chomp chomp." We would visualize the cancer being wiped out. While we knew this seemed juvenile, it was designed to let us think on positive things, it seemed to work, at least in our minds. It was important nothing negative got stuck into our thought process. To get well takes more than medicine. It takes a thought process that is focused and direct. It takes everything.

Meanwhile, it was still a mystery to the radiologists as to the cause of Jim's extreme and unrelenting nausea. The relief provided by the suppository was short lived. We had spoken with most everyone who might be of help. I met with dieticians to get some ideas on helping to control nausea. I got ideas from nurses and from other caregivers. I read everything I could get my hands on.

And then, I read some information that was extremely helpful. Because of the size of the radiation field on his body, they were actually radiating a part of his esophagus. Bingo! There was a logical explanation for his coughing! I spoke with one of the doctors, and he said there could be spasms of the esophagus. And, the radiation was hitting some other organs as well that might cause nausea. His spine was being radiated; that was causing some pain in his back. In other words, he was getting so much radiation; it had to be causing some problems. He was receiving the maximum dosage for his lifetime. He would not be treated with this type of radiation ever again. Each time before treatment the radiologist performed a battery of measurements. This allowed the proper amount of radiation to be administered so his body would get a precise measure. Even one iota too much could be damaging to his body. One day when they were positioning him for treatment Jim said, "That's not the way they did this yesterday."

The radiologist told him, "We are blocking off your spine. It's had all the radiation it can have as of yesterday."

One morning when Jim woke up he seemed worse than usual. He was unable to get out of bed. He refused his bath. He eventually got up and went to the bathroom. He wanted to brush his teeth, but had to rest for a while after using the bathroom before he could brush his teeth. Then he had to rest after brushing his teeth. His appointment for treatment would have to wait a while. I called the hospital and told them he would need to come in an hour or two later. Jim was not doing well, and I wondered if we'd even be able to get him to treatment at all. Finally, by his moving slowly and my being patient to dress him, we got ready went to the appointment. There were only a few more treatments and we'd be going home to Tennessee. I asked the nurse if the doctor could get a look at him before that day's treatment, because of his increased weakness. The doctor saw him and they decided to administer the treatment. I was afraid it might kill him that day.

The next morning he had grown weaker. He wanted to get out of bed but just couldn't do it. I thought of calling an ambulance to get him to the hospital. I did not see how he could take one more radiation treatment. He was thin, pale, and barely breathing. I was not sure exactly what to do, but my head and my heart were both moving toward calling the radiologist. I called. I spoke with his nurse. I told her we would be over in a few minutes if my husband didn't die before we got there. I told her we would need to go directly into the exam room, or I could take him to the ER, whichever did they preferred. He simply could not sit in the waiting room. He could not sit up at all. She asked the questions nurses have to ask, one of them was regarding his appetite.

"Appetite?" I asked. "Really? Yes. He eats. And throws up after every meal; however, if something isn't done, he will be dead before dinner."

I hung up the phone. Ronnie and I scooped Jim up, got him to the car, and broke speed limits to get him to the hospital. There was no place to park. Ronnie just left the car sitting out front. If anyone would have wanted a new Lincoln, they could have had that one that day. We took Jim inside and as we made our way down the red lined hall of burnt flesh smell. We saw the radiologist standing beside the door with his hand outstretched toward the exam room. There was no waiting. Not that day.

He had a look of amazement on his face.

"Mr. Oakley, what happened to you? I just saw you yesterday." He weighed him, listened to his chest and was quiet for a moment. He just looked at us.

"We are going to suspend your treatments for a while. You are too weak to continue them." We had our calendars marked for the last treatment and the day we'd get to go home circled. We were literally counting the days until we could go home. This would keep us in Houston until August.

Jim said, "I don't want to take any longer than I have to with these treatments. We are a long way from home. We have children who need us. We need to get this over with."

By this time we were both starting to cry. The doctor looked helpless.

43

He said, "I want to admit you to the hospital for some fluids. You will feel better then. When you feel better and are hydrated then we will see when we can continue the treatments. You have been strong, but now you are too weak." His voice was kind and sympathetic as he spoke.

We were relieved on some level, just knowing there would be help. He was too weak to have treatments and too weak to travel. We got him admitted quickly and by the next afternoon he was markedly better. A couple of liters of fluid made a big difference. His color was better and his sense of humor was coming back. When we went to the hospital to get him, he said he felt so much better he thought he could carry Ronnie out of the hospital. He was trying to be sure that we still remembered how to laugh. It had been a grueling week.

Treatments resumed. We were almost finished. In a few days we could go home. We had a lot to do, so we made our lists to be sure nothing was forgotten. We had utilities to disconnect, the final bill to pay at the apartment complex, and some packing to do. Mary came back out that last week and helped us as we packed. We were moving again, but this time back to Nashville! We were going home!

Before we left Houston we were to have one last visit with the oncologist. He would be giving us information on chemotherapy. I had seen him caring for Jim and had learned he was a compassionate and wonderful doctor. An oncologist can't give people the hope they want. They have to find it within themselves. At the last meeting with this fine doctor, he laid out the rest of the treatment plan. Six rounds of chemotherapy, but it would be administered in Nashville. We would be seeing a team of oncologists there. The idea of chemotherapy was more frightening to me than I wanted to admit. For months and months we had been rubbing elbows with people who were on chemotherapy. Their pain and misery was all too evident in their pale, see-through skin, bald heads and dark circles under their eyes. They looked so weak that a small puff of wind could literally make them fall over. I had seen Jim weak and truthfully, looking at him, even on a good day, I didn't feel he could live through chemotherapy. I just wanted to take him home and preserve him for a while and let him get stronger. Then I'd let another doctor treat him. He had not been out of my sight for months now and I had practically learned to read his mind. I knew what every facial expression meant, and could predict what he would want to eat for the next meal. I was losing myself, but the new me I found was more self assured and confident. I was trusting God with life - all of it. I couldn't see or touch my children, but I knew God's hand was on them constantly.

There had been twenty eight radiation treatments. Jim had lost fifty one pounds. He was getting stronger, but still looked like a very sick man. We still hadn't been given any hope.

It seemed to me that some doctor would stop by and say, "You are well now. Go have a good life." That never happened. Ever. You just can't trust cancer. Getting well isn't a sure thing. Cancer is a sneak thief of life. We were determined not to go home in fear, but to go home and look forward to many good years. We would not live in constant fear of its return. We just would not!

We returned home the first part of August of 1982 after four months of attention from M.D. Anderson Cancer Center. We were so thankful for their care and mostly for their ability to remove the cancer. The surgery removed the bulk of the tumor and the massive amounts of radiation were administered to the site to destroy any particles that might be left. The selfish prayer I had been praying, that Jim would not need chemotherapy - was a prayer that definitely did not get answered my way. My reasoning was if the cancer was taken away by surgery and the radiation that followed had been a security measure, then that should be enough. I was so afraid that any more treatments would kill my husband. I feared chemotherapy's effects even if it did give us more assurance. Jim had already been through so much. I just wanted our life back. Then I realized… this was our life.

Tennessee never looked better to us! We were home! We noticed every building and every tree on the way from the airport to home. Ramona and Sonny, Jim's sister and her husband, picked us up at the airport in our very own car. We had no idea what was in store for us when we entered our neighborhood. Sonny slowed down so we could have a moment to focus on what was taking place. There were people, family, neighbors and friends from church, standing along the streets waving to us! I would guess there were two hundred people. We felt like royalty! This plan had been masterminded by our dear friends Kitty and B.B. Boyd, Jr. He had announced the plan at church, giving details of when we would be coming home. He encouraged anyone who wanted, to be there to welcome us home. It was a strong visual for them to see the man they'd been praying for and know he was doing well. We were reassured of their love for us at the sight of them.

The moment we saw our house, we could not help but be moved to tears by the larger than life welcome home sign our children had made for us. It was the size of a billboard! Yellow ribbons had been tied around all the trees! It was evident we had been missed. The friends, the sign, yellow ribbons, our children! What a homecoming! We went inside just long enough to step outside onto our front porch and wave to the crowd like royalty. The crowd dispersed, leaving our hearts overflowing with gratitude. We went back inside to enjoy the food and see our children again. We were so happy to be home again. We simply could not take our eyes off our children. The house looked the same, yet different. The joy we felt at being at home again was immeasurable.

We had been home a month. In September we would meet the oncologists in Nashville and discuss chemotherapy. The time we'd had after radiation had given Jim's body an opportunity to become stronger and heal. I was also having him drink dietary supplements to help him regain strength. He would need all the strength he could get. Chemotherapy was to be the next mode of treatment. He was looking better than ever when we went for that September visit.

That was the day we met Dr. Charles McKay. He entered the room much like Kramer on Seinfeld. He was young, very tall and hair wet from a morning swim. He appeared surprised when he looked at Jim, then to me, and back to Jim and said, "You look terrible!"

Oh, that was not a good thing to say to me, Jim's big bad watchdog caregiver.

"He does not! He looks good." I said sharply.

He looked away from me and over at Jim.

"Well, I am the third guy to get a hold of you, and I gotta tell you, you do look rough, and sometimes the chemotherapy can kill you." He said matter-of-factly as he positioned his stethoscope.

"Don't kill this one. He is special," I warned him, harshly.

"They all are," He whispered kindly, as he gently placed the stethoscope on Jim's back.

"Hmmm, that went well." I thought, making mental note to get rid of this doctor and find someone else. He was just a kid anyway. What was he, twenty? It was for sure I was feeling older than my years.

Chemotherapy was to begin immediately. The first chemo treatment would be done at the hospital. Jim and I decided on Monday for treatment day. I conducted sales meetings each Monday and it would be a time we both could get our business done and have the next few days with those details behind us.

The day of the first scheduled treatment, Jim and I drove to the hospital, admitted him, and I went home to make dinner. I made a huge pot of spaghetti sauce for the children and summoned cousin Lori, their student mother to come and stay with them as she had so many times over the last few months. I set the table, finished preparing the food and got dressed for my Mary Kay meeting. It would be held across town at the office of my Senior Director (now Sue McGray).

It began to rain just as I left my driveway. It was a huge thunderstorm with dark rolling clouds, suggesting there was more to come. Suddenly I realized I could not deal with the meeting. I could not make myself smile or motivate anybody tonight. I drove to Sue's home, where the meeting was being held and told everyone I wasn't able to stay. I had to go to the hospital to be with Jim. They agreed. I should be with him. I left and drove toward Centennial Medical Center. I wasn't even sure how to get there, even though I had been earlier in the day. I was consumed with fear, guilt and shame that I had even tried to get back to normal so quickly. It just felt wrong and I hated myself for my stupidity. I was lost in downtown Nashville somewhere in the middle of a rain storm.

I found the hospital somehow. Driving around in circles helped. I even found a parking place. Each victory made me stronger. I was amazed I was able to find his room. When I opened the door, there he was, in the dark, all hooked up to chemo drugs, turned toward the window. The storm was still making its presence known with constant thunder and blinding sheets of rain. I walked over to the side of his bed. He turned slowly, smiled and said, in Big Bopper style, "Hellllo baby, I knew you'd be here. You couldn't make it without me, could you?"

I pulled a chair over as close to his bed as I could get.

"No, I couldn't." I said, reaching out to touch his face.

I knew I was where I needed to be. I called home to check on the children.

Lori was able to stay overnight with Greg and Kristy. In the morning I brought Jim home. He had made it through the first chemo treatment. He had only one treatment in the hospital. Each treatment after that was done at Dr. McKay's office. We never were apart again at treatment time.

I have blocked some things totally from my mind, because I have no recollection of taking him for the other treatments. I know I did, but I can't envision Dr. McKay's office at that time. I have no memory of the treatment rooms. I do not remember driving him. I do remember being at home with him after the treatments. I have just enough memory of the first time around of chemotherapy for it to have burned indelible holes into my heart and mind. They were too painful and I have needed no recall of them, so they are gone. I don't want them back.

I do remember each time as we'd come home from chemo, Jim would be nauseated and immensely ill for three days. There was nothing I could do. At the end of three days he would be ready for a bowl of chicken noodle soup and a glass of buttermilk (I know, yuck!). But that combination seemed to be just exactly what his body needed. As treatments went on, he would get nauseated more quickly and finally toward the end of the course of treatment, he would just throw up in the waste basket in the treatment room. I do remember seeing the huge needle filled with a red medicine, adriamycin, the one they call The Red Death, and I left the room before it was administered. During those months and for a time afterward, I could not have a bottle of ketchup in Jim's line of vision, nor could I serve spaghetti sauce. Red stuff brought on his nausea.

The day his hair began to fall out was a most traumatic day for both of us. He was having breakfast and hair began to drop out all over his shoulders. He pushed back his plate and stopped eating. We both did. When he got into the shower, he watched the rest of his hair go down the drain. Back then, in 1982, bald wasn't yet beautiful. Hair was. We both cried most all of that day. He had dark circles under his eyes and he was pale. And now he was almost bald. He looked and felt awful. His skin became unnaturally soft, baby soft. He hardly needed to shave. The things we dreaded were happening. He looked sicker than any sick person I'd ever seen. He had been so healthy and so handsome. We had to find hope and thankfulness in this, but it was hard. The only thing we could be thankful for was that it wasn't one of our children with this horrible disease. We had seen so many little children with the chemo side effects, and unless they were having a really bad sick day, they were smiling. We worked on smiling after the incident of the hair falling out. So many people were praying for us and we knew we would get through it, but it was a rough time. I am glad for the blocked memory of much of it. I don't want to remember that pain. Neither of us wants the memories back, but enough of it lingers so we don't lose our compassion for others. We endured and God helped us through. Our prayers for others who battle cancer are more than genuine. We hurt along with them. Their pain is part ours.

Before the chemotherapy was completed, Jim's hair began to come back. His color improved slightly and he began to gain some weight. The hope we were hanging onto was proving itself to be real. Tests indicated that the surgery and treatments had killed the cancer; it was gone. It had been a long road from diagnosis to now. We were so grateful for our new start! He was going to be well. We'd continue to have check ups here in Nashville with Dr. McKay. And yes, I did learn to appreciate Dr. McKay. It didn't take long for me to see he was absolutely the doctor God knew we needed. We have him at the top of our list of heroes. We have seen him in action.

Jim went back to work in 1985. He had stringent restrictions regarding his limited lung capacity. The surgery, radiation and chemotherapy had taken a toll on him, but his determination, and our prayers for him to be able to be back with us seemed to work. He made a dramatic come back. It took five years for him to feel well, but he was cancer-free and we were in the process of making life great again for the four of us. We were done fighting, at least for a while.

CHAPTER 8

Life as We Knew It

The next twenty seven years went by much too quickly. Our children grew up as we did the things that families do. We celebrated birthdays in huge ways and had Christmases that were always fun and different. We made our own personal family Christmas themes during times when things were not the picture perfect holiday postcard. We saw both children graduate from high school and go to college, each of them coping with the things of life that have helped to shape them into the absolutely wonderful adults they now are. We had weddings, grandchildren and a divorce here and there.

Life is never full of just the good stuff. I used to wonder why it was like that. It gave me headaches. I stopped taking advice from the people with whom I'd never want to exchange places. I stopped having headaches. We all have to learn life lessons, and sometimes it just hurts and hurts. God helps us through and if we are able to muster enough courage to go on, we emerge a stronger edition of ourselves. We must learn cherish the good days, the days when the chaos isn't there. The days when pain and suffering and remorse aren't accompanying us are the bright and shiny days. Somehow those days get overlooked because they seem uneventful. If we are constantly looking ahead for some other part of life to happen, we miss out on today.

Our children have grown up strong and confident. They are talented and probably wise beyond their years now. They grew up in a happy home. We had all but the picket fence. We did have a good life with them. It just went by too quickly.

One of the things I prayed for back in 1982, in our life of the first cancer diagnosis, was that Jim would be able to live to see our children grow up. I audaciously asked God for a couple of grandchildren. It made me feel rooted and grounded in a plan for the future that included Jim. It was a way to tie us together forever. We are blessed to have three grandchildren at this time in our lives. We have two granddaughters and one grandson. Morgan, Mallory and Corbin. Each one is beautiful/handsome, talented, kind hearted, loving and precious to us. Really, not just to us, but to everyone they meet. We could not be more proud. We are a family blessed beyond belief!

Jim retired from Ford Glass Plant in 2001. He worked sixteen years and was able to retire. During some of those years he worked a lot of overtime, working more hours than I felt he should have. His work wasn't hard on him because the people he worked for were graciously understanding of his health situation. He had good co-workers on his jobs. They more than likely picked up more work and did it to ease Jim's load. Several of those men are still good friends today. Jim Hall was one of those coworkers. One day the two of them were talking. Jim Oakley said to Jim Hall, "I don't know why God let me stay around so long."

Jim Hall didn't hesitate. He said, "I know why!" Their friendship and Jim's Christian influence was in great part the reason Jim Hall became a Christian. We treasure the friendship of Jim and his wife, Nancy.

I have summed up twenty-seven years with so few words. It was my plan to do so. During those years, we experienced the ups and downs of life just as anyone else has. We had begun our journey of growing old together and had entered into our golden years. Our hair began turning silver and we had now been married for over forty years. We had weathered enough storms together to be known as pretty good navigators. We'd managed to hang onto the boat and never bailed out. We'd always noticed the sunshine after the rain. When there is a rainbow, we think about the promise that the rainstorms aren't going to be what destroys us.

"We know that God is able to give us grace, so that in all things, at all times, we will have what we need, and we will abound in every good work," II Corinthians 9:8.

From my journal 2007:

"We depend on God to give us what we need. We ask for little on a daily basis, but praise Him a lot for what He does for us. When we go through a crisis, we don't feel guilty for going to Him boldly over and over petitioning him, begging him for what we want. He knows I will not stop asking. He knows I will not stop thanking Him. He knows I accept that His way is best and His timing means everything, but still I want my way and His way to be the same. It will not work out my way every time. I know that. He knows I know. He made me. I get it."

The upper respiratory infections were frequent and each episode was followed far too closely by another. Jim was sick almost constantly. He was tired and irritable. He didn't sleep well. It was like 1982 again. I was seeing the same patterns emerge. It all felt too familiar. He was having check ups, but I was the only one seeing the red flags. Jim questioned my intuition, but I never did. Intuition is God-given. It may bring the answers we get when we pray for guidance. If we pray for guidance, then we'd better fasten our seat belts!

We owe a debt of gratitude to Vanderbilt University Medical Center, specifically the wonderful doctors and nurse practitioners in the allergy sinus program, for helping me see that I wasn't crazy for pursuing these symptoms. I had seen a program on television for people with chronic allergy and sinus symptoms. I called and got Jim an appointment. If his symptoms were allergy related and not a recurrence, I believed they would be the ones to address these problems. I wanted him to be well.

They diagnosed a mass in one of his sinuses which proved to be a dangerous fungal infection. Treatment began, including surgery to clear it away. We both felt relieved. After surgery, recovery and new meds, the old symptoms returned. He was losing weight and just looked sick. Our doctors there were quite concerned and could see why I was becoming almost frantic. It was heartbreaking when the nurse practitioner told us she and the other doctors there felt the cancer may have recurred. I think everyone in the room that day shed a tear or two. It was time to schedule an appointment with Dr. McKay. The allergy and sinus part had been handled. We had been in good hands.

Jim had continued seeing Dr. McKay for yearly visits these last twenty seven years. He and my husband had bonded.

They enjoyed talking about hunting and fishing. I didn't feel the need to make every visit with Jim. A yearly check up with the oncologist had become routine for us. When I'd hear the report was good, I felt my prayers had been answered. I would occasionally show up at the appointment just to make sure they were really doing blood work and not just talking hunting and fishing. When he'd enter the treatment room and I'd be sitting there with Jim, Dr. McKay would say, "Oh, you brought the Boss today."

It was a good feeling to be getting cancer-free reports all these years. One of us would always make a comment regarding our thankfulness about the cancer having stayed away. We all felt we had beaten it, but not enough to ignore the possibility that it might rear its ugly head again. While our friendly banter took place, we were still watchful and cautious.

The x rays were normal for a guy with one lung missing. The blood work was normal. Despite these yearly checkups, some miniscule cancer cells must have been hiding and were just now showing themselves to be present. Scans had been done, and there had been some abnormalities, such as a spot in the right chest cavity. It seemed to be calcified. I have never ever been a patient person, and I didn't want to wait to see if the spot changed. It had been sitting there for a while with no changes. I had insisted upon a fine needle aspiration to determine if cancer cells were present. The doctor and I talked about the risks and benefits of such an invasive test. We were sent to a lung specialist. I continued to insist on the test. None of the doctors thought it to be a good idea. I felt outnumbered, but didn't feel like quitting.

The doctor assured me he would do the biopsy if Jim agreed on it. I was for it! I was overruled by Jim. He agreed with the doctors. He wanted to go fishing. I was not trying to be rude to Jim or to the doctors. I just had this gut feeling. Nothing was showing up in the blood work. As I acquiesced, I was still determined to find out what was in Jim's chest. He'd go fishing and I would try my best to simmer down, but I wouldn't quit.

I didn't think it was a good idea, anyway, to have the biopsy and then go fishing. Not a good idea to be around foreign germs with a hole poked in his side! I could only imagine infection! People die from less. Jim said he felt better and the symptoms did seem to have disappeared. The antibiotics had given him a false sense of security. I hushed and Jim went fishing. I was irritated, thinking of the precious time we were losing as this monster loomed larger on our horizon. I believe I stayed irritated for two years. Jim's words echoed in my head from that stormy night in 1982, something about my being crazy. Once again I knew I wasn't crazy, but I wondered why I had this guttural feeling that he needed this biopsy. I was tired of the sound of my own thoughts.

We scheduled an appointment for the following week with Dr. McKay. A needle biopsy was performed on April 1, 2009 at Baptist Hospital. Dr. McKay met with us a few days later. He came into the exam room where we anxiously awaited the results he was going to give. He closed the door, sat down and looked shocked.

He said, "I have some odd news."

I thought *odd* was an odd choice of words. He continued, sensing the questioning look I was giving him.

"Odd is the only way to describe this. I am floored. This is thymoma again. It is back."

We thought we'd never hear those words again. Jim had been cancer free for twenty-seven years. Dr. McKay went on to tell us that this just never happens. We knew we had been one of the fortunate ones. For those few moments we were all in shock. We just sat there. Since our shock was newer than Dr. McKay's, he felt like talking. Jim and I had no hard reaction to this; we just faced it head on. No crying, mostly shock. I asked Dr. McKay what the next step would be. He said he had already spoken with oncologists at M.D. Anderson in Houston.

He had told them, "I'll send you any information you need on this guy, test results, whatever, I'll even send you the guy!" And so that is what we collectively decided to do. We would go to M.D. Anderson for their part in Jim's treatment plan. Dr. McKay would work with them and would administer chemotherapy if it was warranted. He didn't know if they would want to do surgery first or not. It didn't really seem likely; however, it could be an option. Dr. McKay told us Jim would more than likely benefit from chemotherapy. All I wanted to hear was the cancer was operable or treatable. We thanked our good doctor, feeling blessed to have him, yet dreading the start of another cancer relationship. We made our plans to travel to Houston. The appointment would be on April 21, 2009.

We never know what is going on inside our bodies. The body has certain symptoms that will begin to play out if we only watch and listen. Take nothing for granted. Dismiss nothing as unimportant. If a problem continues, it is a warning something is abnormal. If it cannot be helped by discontinuing a food, beverage, or medicine, or with more rest, more exercise, or drinking more water, see a doctor. If you feel something is wrong, it probably is. I think my intuition is hardwired into my brain so tightly that I cannot ignore my feelings when something is wrong, or right. And in my husband's case, it has made all the difference in the world.

It was the same type of cancer as before, malignant thymoma. Twenty-seven years ago it was Stage IV, meaning that it had metastasized to at least one organ. This time, twenty seven years later, tests showed it was confined to the right chest area where his lung had been removed. I asked a nurse what stage we would consider this to be. She shrugged and said she thought a recurrence was stage IV. We decided it didn't matter. It was back and it was mean. We would fight it. The remaining lung was not affected. At least the monster had the decency to leave his remaining lung alone. We could count that as a blessing.

On the way home from Dr. McKay's office that day we decided how we would handle this. We would first tell our children and grandchildren, and then the rest of the family. We would have it announced it at church. We would get all the prayers going we could get. It worked last time. I hated this diagnosis but I knew the doctors would know what to do. Between Dr. McKay and the Houston doctors we would have the best care available. We would give this cancer a real fight once again. I prayed for another victory over cancer.

As the time for our trip to Houston drew near, it was suggested by Rhonda Hodges, Jim's niece, we set up a blog site. It was a place to keep everyone updated on Jim's condition, as well as receive encouraging words from readers. It sounded great to me. I mentioned it to my friend Debbie Davis, who immediately took care of setting up a site for us, emailed me the web address and my password. Perfect. No one would have to wonder what was happening. I would update often. We would, however, continue to follow our same protocol when new information was received. Our children would know first, next our grandchildren and then the others. The last time around, twenty-seven years ago, our son and daughter lived this nightmare as children. Now they were adults and would have to do it all again.

A cancer diagnosis changes your life. There are many appointments and a lot of waiting. At the end of the day, you find yourself quite exhausted. You must find ways to limit activities that drain you. There is physical and mental strain. The last thing that you want to do is relay the same information over and over. Using this blog site kept me from having to make phone calls and re-live the news each time. I enjoyed posting and stepping away from the computer. More was saved than just the items I wrote and posted. I felt some stress relief as I wrote. Once I became adept at using the site, I felt a mental release. It was therapeutic.

The comments on the blog from friends and family always cheered us on. It was wonderful to visit the site and see how many people had cared enough not only to read Jim's story, but to post encouraging words for us. It was also nice to hear that people enjoyed my writing. I've always written, mostly for fun. Several people asked me to put our story into book form. Perhaps you are one of my encouragers. Thank you.

CHAPTER 9

A Warm Send Off

Jim's family is large. It would be safe to say that he is one of the favorites, if not the actual favorite. It was only fitting and proper they would give us a warm send off to Houston the night before we left.

It was Sunday night, April 19, 2009. We met at Lori and Charlie Simms's home, Jim's niece and her husband. They opened their beautiful home to the family and a few close friends for one of the most memorable nights of our lives.

Our hearts were once again filled with gratitude for each family member and friend who came to pray with us before we left for Houston. Each prayer was fervent and power-packed with belief that God would heal Jim. We cherish each person who prayed that night. The prayers of Michelle Gossett Lasley and her brother Gavin Gossett were so riveting, so sincere and overflowing with love. They prayed audaciously, yet ever so respectfully, petitioning God to heal their Uncle Jim. Their prayers helped us feel confident that God was listening. The Lord was truly in that place that night. Not a person there would deny it. Our spirits were high. Our hearts were full. Our bags were packed, in true Oakley fashion, with way too much stuff. We were ready to go.

As we left Lori and Charlie's that night, some of our girls had packed away goodies in Ronnie's vehicle for us to enjoy along the road (including, but not limited to, a variety of homemade cookies, peanut butter fudge, the entire contents of a vending machine, and even some homemade jelly). When Ronnie came to pick us up the next morning, we couldn't help but laugh at the tiny space left for me to sit in the back seat. There was just so much stuff! Stuff we needed for our journey to Texas. We were a rolling snack bar!

As I opened cards and read them aloud to Jim and Ronnie, I'd pass goodies up to them. They'd interrupt my reading only to make a request to pass more candy or cookies. The copious amount of notes and treats provided concrete evidence that we were loved, and loved a lot. One of the biggest surprises in opening the goody packages came when I discovered our family photo album. I wanted a picture of Jim and me with our grandchildren. Rhonda photographed us and then compiled all the photos into an over-the-top album. She far succeeded my expectations, and her thoughtfulness in surprising us with this album for our trip was precious. It never hurts to have a professional photographer in the family.

Yet another tear-jerker tucked in the treasure trove came from our daughter Kristy. She had taken a blank journal and secretly passed it around at our church for people to write messages for us—kind words, well wishes, promises of prayer. That little book will always be one of our most cherished possessions. It was a precious thing for our daughter to do. What a loving act of kindness!

We were on our way to Houston again, Ronnie driving us, to find out if the cancer could be removed once again. We were all twenty-seven years older and in some ways wiser. We would handle the outcome together whatever the answer. As Ronnie drove with Jim sitting in the shotgun position, I took out my journal and began to write:

April 20, 2009: *"So this must be real. I thought it might be a mini-nightmare. We are on our way to Houston again after all these years. My mind is running faster than the speed limit. I can barely scribble or think, but want to keep a few things in mind about our trip. This time I could lose Jim. I cannot imagine my life without him. I need the doctors to tell us they can make him well again."*

We arrived at our Houston hotel just before dark. The suite was perfect for the three of us. The hotel provided breakfast, a shuttle to the hospital and snacks in the evening, all complimentary. The staff was friendly and this hotel seemed to be a place where many families of cancer patients stayed. It's not the best of circumstances to make new friends, and each of you is more than aware of that. You nod in agreement and share your stories, and for those few moments you are in a cocoon where everyone understands without having to voice it. You find that you are all in a battle with some description of the monster, and to learn about each other's fight helps to strengthen all involved. None of us wants to be this tough, but unfortunately, the tough times make us the strongest.

Jim's appointment was set for April 21 at M.D. Anderson. We were elated at the changes to the facility. Where there had been concrete, there were trees and sidewalks and fountains and beautiful sitting areas. It was a tropical paradise of wonder! The parking lot we'd walked across every day when we were here in 1982 was now transformed into a winding wonder of tropical landscaping that would make a garden club jealous! The hotel where we stayed in 1982 was no longer there, but now a series of beautiful modern buildings stood in its place, including a new hotel for patients and their families. This new campus didn't have a typical hospital feel. Our moods lightened as we drove around the area. The place was magnificent! It was just beautiful!

As soon as we stepped into the main entrance of the hospital, we were in a bright cheerful lobby with a snack bar, a library and a gift shop. The aroma of flavored coffees filled the air. There were friendly staff members to direct us where we needed to go. There were comfortable chair sections strategically placed. There were fountains and plants and gigantic fish tanks and carpet and bright sculptures everywhere! The atmosphere was warm and welcoming. Each floor of the hospital's common areas had a new coordinating inviting décor with even more comfortable chairs. In most areas you'd see jigsaw puzzles in process. It was obvious the issue of comfort and beauty while waiting had been addressed. There were several designated areas staffed by former cancer patients who were there to pour you a fresh cup of coffee or hot chocolate and serve you cookies. Jim always knew where to find me if we got separated. I'd be in the nearest cookie room. I loved hearing from other patients— their stories of hope and life. I began to crave the knowledge that the cancer monster was being annihilated. I wanted to hear success stories. The cookies didn't hurt either.

We were overwhelmed at the positive changes at the hospital. It is still operating as a well-oiled machine with a big ole heart. Would you believe they have a place where you can take a nap and they will give you a warm blanket? These improvements we now enjoyed all these years later extended the joy in our hearts for M.D. Anderson. Fears are easier handled in an environment such as this. The beauty and comfort took the hospital feel away. It had the look of a luxury hotel!

Jim's tests began and were extensive. We saw one of the thoracic surgeons who would present Jim's case to the tumor board the following Tuesday. He began the tests with a pulmonary function evaluation to see how his lung was performing. Should surgery be an option, it would be crucial for him to be able to breathe on his own once the respirator was removed. He had blood work, x-rays and scans. After all these tests, we would return home and await the outcome. We would soon know if there would be surgery or chemotherapy or both. We'd be leaving for home as soon as the doctor's visits were done for the day. No use waiting here in Texas for results that would be given to us in four days. With Big Ron as our chauffeur, we wouldn't see the sun go down in Texas. As Big Ron says about driving, "It's something I can do."

We were quickly Tennessee bound. We knew this needed to be a fast trip. Yeah, I know. I'd have flown. Jim doesn't like to fly. We arrived back home in Nashville at four a.m. We had another safe journey behind us. We would be home only a few days then return to Houston to meet with the doctor and learn the test results.

Our prayers were for Jim to be healed of this disease once again. We both felt the prayers of many, many people. I'd tried to use the blog site but felt uptight about sharing personal feelings. I developed writer's block. Me? I have loved writing since I was a child! Each time I'd sit down to write I'd get the deer in the headlight stare. Not until I heard from several people that our friends and family were waiting for the updates did I feel the writer's block lift. It became easier to post. Readers were encouraging. Writing once again became my therapy.

April 28, 2009 *"Our hearts are made glad as we read your good wishes toward us. We feel your prayers! How else could we venture into this unknown void of cancer for the second time without a major crash and burn? Thank you for petitioning God on our behalf.*

We are taking a last look around home for a little while. We leave for Houston again in the morning. I was walking around our yard, drinking in the beauty of every iris bloom, I was thinking about how we love our homes here on earth, especially the times we are looking at the beauty and not the dust of it all. How often do we stop and take time to enjoy the beauty in our lives? Our homes on earth are worthy of that attention, but our fast paced lives prevent us from realizing the sheer joy of the beauty that is ours. I don't want to miss a thing! I was amazed at the army of roses that arrived to greet me this morning. Yesterday, only a bunch tiny buds, today, hundreds of roses in bloom. I guess they knew I might not be here to see them before they wilted away. Can we even imagine a fraction of the beauty of our mansion in Heaven? As we see the beauty around us, not just our physical homes, and the nature that surrounds us, but in the people we love most dearly. Our precious families and our dear friends notice them and tell them you love them. Our families are people we sometimes take for granted. Don't."

We will miss our children and grandchildren most while we are gone, but will be in touch by phone. My prayer is that all of you who love us take care of them. Pray for them. Hug them. Give them encouragement too. We await good news, but the scary part is the not knowing. We do fine with an action plan, but the not knowing part, that place where faith is all we have, please pray we make it to the place where faith is all we need."

April 30, 2009: "We had another safe trip to Houston. We were ready for rest. Five am came at its usual early time. The doctor's appointment was scheduled for seven thirty am; however, as we were traveling, we received a call from the nurse practitioner. She said the doctor had asked for more pulmonary function tests and to go there at six thirty am. Once those tests were done we saw the surgeon around noon. It made for a full day.

During some of our waiting, Jim said, 'We haven't heard any of the doctors say 'no problem' but we haven't heard anyone say 'no hope'. We still have a problem, but we do have hope."

When we lose hope, we lose energy and it is impossible to fight this battle before us without both. My prayer has been for this cancer to be operable. That prayer has been answered so far. I am humbled beyond measure."

May 2, 2009: "We are home again! We had constant sunshine yesterday as we traveled and no rain last night. We arrived home at one am.

We met with another of his doctors yesterday. He reviewed results of the tumor board and gave us final test results. Another prayer was answered when he told us the tumors were confined to the chest wall and seems to be the direct site of origination with no metastasis. We are thankful to know more about the enemy. We are ready to fight. It is the consensus of the physicians that three to four rounds of chemotherapy be administered. Chemotherapy will be done in Nashville. We will return to Houston after the second round of chemo to see how the tumor is responding. That will determine if surgery will be done. Plans to continue the treatment plan will be based on those findings. While this cancer is rare, it does have a history of responding to the treatment they are suggesting. Patients have actually been cured of it. We've come a long way since 1982.''

We were told that Jim does actually hold a record, twenty seven years for a non recurrent malignant thymoma. Most of them return in just a few months.

Thymoma is a disease in which malignant cancer cells form on the outside surface of the thymus. The thymus, a small organ that lies in the upper chest under the breastbone, is part of the lymph system. Many times the symptoms go unnoticed until the tumor has grown considerably. Possible signs of thymoma include fatigue, shortness of breath, cough and chest pain. It is important to never disregard any symptom that persists. However, sometimes there are no symptoms. The cancer may be discovered during a routine chest x-ray. Further testing may be conducted to identify a thymoma.

On May 4, 2009, I contacted Dr. McKay's office. They had received the information from M.D. Anderson regarding test results and suggestions for treatment. While this wasn't one of the most pleasant projects to get rolling, it was one that needed to be done quickly. I could not stand to have one more day pass to let this cancer grow. We had an appointment for blood work scheduled for the following morning; and on May 6 at five thirty am we would go to Baptist Hospital to have his port-a-cath installed. Would that be the word to use when they insert a tube into the great vein near your heart? It is an easier way to administer and receive the chemotherapy, although it sounds horribly frightening. The days flew by, although we weren't counting them with excited anticipation of something we'd be doing for fun. We were going to Baptist Hospital to have his port installed. Once again, we were entering into the world of cancer treatment. We had a lot to do to prepare.

While we were at Baptist, he also had an EEG to check on his heart. We stayed around for a few hours for observation. We later met with Dr. McKay and discussed the treatment schedule. He did a fine job in 1982 of helping Jim to get well. We knew he would do it again. Last time he got a guy who looked terrible. This time he got a guy who felt well most of the time and didn't look sick. With the innumerable advances in cancer treatment for the last twenty seven years, we felt this whole ordeal would be easier for Jim's body to tolerate. Our confidence in our doctors was unwavering, but I felt small and helpless. Jim realized I was feeling afraid. He told me he believed I could do anything, and this was just one more mountain we would climb together.

CHAPTER 10

Scared and Alone

The world is amazingly still at four am. It is also quite dark. We arrived at Baptist Hospital at five am to have the port-a-cath installed. We were taken to a nice warm room on the fifth floor. It was unseasonably cold that morning for May. It is always cold in the hospitals, no matter the season. Good germ control. Our view of the dark rainy sky made me want to arm wrestle Jim for the bed, but I was afraid I'd get the port, so I took the cold leather chair and gave him the warm blanketed bed. We had been in the room five minutes when they came to take him to have an echo cardiogram. They needed to see how his heart muscles were acting before chemotherapy. The test showed his heart strong enough to endure treatment.

The sun didn't shine that day. It was misty, dark and rainy all day long. When the attendant came to take Jim to surgery, he allowed me to walk along beside the gurney. He said he'd show me a place to wait nearby. I walked along holding Jim's hand. He made his usual funny remarks and I did my best to laugh. As we neared the surgical area, we saw our medical team waiting for us. We introduced all around, looked at wrist bands and name badges and entered a room not needing a view. They rolled Jim into the room, placed the gurney under a bright light and left the door open. I stood awkwardly in the hallway waiting for my cue to leave. The doctor motioned me to come over to the gurney. After the doctor showed us the device and explained the placement and function, it was time to begin. The doctor invited me to stay during the procedure. I thanked him profusely, but given my propensity to fainting, I told him I'd pass. I hoped someone would wave me away like a fly. But no, they continued to give me more information than I would ever need concerning this apparatus that would be installed into my husband's upper chest for the rest of his life. I listened; saw the item that they would install including the tools they'd do it with. All I could hear was the sound of my ears ringing. My heart was still in my chest cavity, because I could feel it pounding. Someone from across the gurney asked if I was okay.

Jim looked at me and said, "Oh, she's fine. She's tough." I stood there listening, smiling and nodding. Someone said it was time to begin. I needed to find the door now, or I'd be under the gurney. I wondered why Jim kept telling everyone I was tough. Like a badge of courage I wear or something. I felt more like a wet potato chip.

"Ok, let me give him a kiss and I'll get out of the way." I said confidently.

One of the nurses touched me on the arm and guided me toward the door. He motioned toward a chair in the hallway and told me to sit. I plopped into the chair like a dog, following the command. He said he'd be right back. He returned with a soft drink.

"Here, drink this honey. You are as white as a little ole ghost. Why, I thought you were gonna faint dead out in there and that doctor had the nerve to keep on talking. You can go wait in his room. He'll be fine and dandy."

Ahhhh…a friend! Anyway, that red can of cool bubbliness was my salvation right then. I was almost sure I'd never tasted one better. I clutched it with both hands, drinking in tiny sips hoping the sobs wouldn't come out and interrupt this sweet relief. I contemplated what the day would bring. I went back to Jim's room and waited.

After about two hours they brought him back to the room. We got him settled in the warm and cozy bed. He would need to be closely monitored for a few hours. We enjoyed some coffee and were served lunch. We stayed on for observation until just before three that afternoon. I was happy to be able to find my car in the parking garage this time without the help of security. Jim was surprised to hear it rumble into the patient pick up area in the same hour that I went to get it.

We drove over to Dr. McKay's office to finalize the treatment plan. The first chemo would begin the upcoming Monday morning. Treatment would take about three hours and would be administered in the doctor's clinic. The drugs used would be much the same as the drugs used before.

It isn't often I say how I really feel. Normally when asked, I use the classic comeback "fine" like all good southern women who know that "how are you" is a greeting and not an invitation to unload your every ailment. I am going to tell you how I really felt on May 6, 2009. It may be helpful. It may not affect anyone else like I was affected that day, but for the record, here goes: An excerpt from my private journal:

"My heart hurts…not my physical heart. My soul… the pit of my being and yet I know that this is just the

beginning of the pain, once again. We spend our young lives rushing forward toward something...the future...maturity... retirement...what? Then we get to a point that seems to have a "no return" sign posted just behind us. We want to back pedal to a time that was better. I can't remember not being concerned for his life. We've always had each other. He still has me. I don't know if I'll always have him, but he will always have me. I know this disease has him again. I feel it pulling him away from me. It can take him away, even if we fight it. It can still take him away. Being strong, oh I am so good at it. I hate this facade. I am not strong. I am not ok. Where are my friends? Who are my friends? They sit with each other and cluck about how sad this is... this cancer Jim has. They take turns burning up the phone lines comforting one another. Where is the comfort that I need? "Why, I am just fine." Like a well-mannered little southern belle. I am fine. They whine and chat and share the details of my life, and then they eat pie.

Alone is easier. On some level, past the cynicism and the bitterness that causes me to make this silent guttural scramble of words of today, there really does exist the of God's perfect companionship. I have a place where trust is genuine, a trust that is worth something lasting and solid. He will fill the emptiness of my soul. He will protect me from all the things I cannot endure. He will not let those things happen to me. He will help me through the times when I dredge up absurdities of this life, when I hide in this cavern of darkness for safety. He will forgive me when I recall painful times that make me hateful to myself. Lord, not even the fake friends are anywhere to be found today, not even out *of duty. It is early yet. Guilt travels mob style. I don't look for any of them."*

This was a tough day for the caregiver. I wished I had not been alone. And yes, cancer is grief personified! One of the grief stages is anger. We deal with it and we move on. It's not healthy to keep it. You have to pray it out, walk it out or talk it out, or all three.

As we drove home from the hospital Jim asked me to make some potato soup like my grandmother, Meme, used to make. That soup was exactly what I was thinking of making for him. Meme's potato soup is a get well potion. Add some crisp cornbread and a long rest in his comfy chair. Those are some of the good things in life that help make him feel better. We are a positive team and we are on a get well mission.

After today's procedure, he would need twenty-four hours to rest. The physical therapy would start in two weeks. If we must prepare for battle, we must plan to go in strong! He has to feel good and be tough enough to fight.

I do not want anyone to think I am super human, or that I never fall apart. I am not always tough. I am not as strong as my husband thinks I am. I've always felt when we do something, we should do it well. Sometimes I do fall apart, just never where anyone can see it. I've never had anyone show up for my pity parties. It would be odd for me to send out invitations. Negative emotions don't get to stay here for long! Fall apart if you must. Fall down if you have to. Get up and find a way to go on. There will be enough crises in life to test us. We don't need to create them.

On May 11 we had a bit of a set back. In my world, a set back is merely a set up for a come back! We showed up for the first treatment. Jim was retaining fluid and it was worrisome as to why. They sent us over to Baptist Hospital for a CT scan. This was not a good time to begin fluid retention. The scan didn't reveal anything that should make us hold treatments, so they would begin immediately.

The night before, I sent out a special prayer request for him via our blog:

"It is time for a specific prayer request. Jim will begin his first course of chemo in the morning at nine. We will be in the doctor's office for three hours. I need you to pray for him. When these cancer killing drugs are infused into his body, pray for the poison to zap the cancer with full force! We want it reduced, dissolved, killed, and just plain gone! I need you to pray that he will not have horrible nausea side effects and he will be strong enough to handle these treatments and get well. We know how his body reacted to chemo in 1982. The drugs will be mostly the same. We know these drugs annihilated the cancer for twenty seven years. However it is you normally pray, pray harder. It is a time to get audacious and boldly ask, believing God will answer in a positive way. I need you to pray him through tomorrow and then I will update you once we get home."

Jim was able to receive his first treatment of chemotherapy for this recurrence on May 12, 2009. Prior to the chemotherapy, we saw the doctor to be sure the fluid retention scare was over. He told us there were no problems showing up on the CT scan of yesterday, nor any reason to suspend treatment any longer. A nice weight loss told us the fluid was dissipating. None of us wanted to delay treatment. Not to treat was not an option. There was nothing to gain by putting treatment off.

Before the chemo began, there was a class for us so we could learn about the drugs, how they would be administered and their side effects. Spouses were invited to stay in the room during treatment. The room was bright with lots of windows, and the nurses had a friendly and cheerful approach as they tended to patients. They did their best to make this experience manageable. This was not what any of us would pick for a day out.

Jim's treatment consisted of three major drugs: cisplatin, cytoxin and adriamycin. With those drugs, he received certain meds to counteract nausea and other problems encountered with chemotherapy. He was given an injection at the end of each course of treatment to help with his blood counts. The first two drugs were administered in the treatment center and the last, adriamycin, would be administered at home through the port in his chest. He wore a computerized pump and it timed the dose into his system. This continued a few days, and then we would go into the doctor's office for the disconnection of the pump from his port. The following day he'd receive the injection to help keep his blood count within good range. If the white blood cells got dangerously low, he would be at greater risk for infection. He has been susceptible to infections for a while, since the removal of his thymus gland in 1982. When his counts were low he would need to stay away from crowds in order to avoid anyone who may have a cough or cold. As the computer ticked away on his side sending death to the cancer cells, I would think of something to say to it. One afternoon there was a plastic toy sword of Corbin's nearby. I picked it up, extended it into the air and said, "We send death to you, thymoma monster! We got you once and we will get you again. Take that!"

I didn't realize Jim was asleep.

"What?" he asked, looking a little startled by my sudden soliloquy.

"What." I replied, dropping the sword onto the floor. It was just some positive visualization. We would not let fear of this cancer get the best of us. We exchanged fear for hope, many times.

An excerpt from my journal: I was feeling a bit like Renaissance woman.

"Never entertain fear. It is a ferocious guest. It will drain you of your best wine and make a mockery of your hospitality. Better to entertain hope, a gracious guest who will sip politely, speak gently and praise your efforts."

The first treatment for the recurrence went well. He had a long nap and when he woke, he told me he'd like to go to Ronnie's for their weekly card game. I drove him to Ronnie's and later, Fred Williams, our neighbor and good friend, brought him home around midnight. Jim and I went downstairs to my office to read the most recent blog posts from friends. I was surprised when he looked at me and told me I looked tired. I might have looked tired, but when is feeling well, I am energized; then I work until I fall over. We went back upstairs and I made his comfy chair nest for him and the cancer killing chemo machine so he could read for a while. Sleep was what I needed.

Morning came too quickly. We had an early appointment for the second day of treatment. Dr. McKay asked Jim how his treatment went.

"It was like a birthday party compared to that first one twenty seven years ago. I did great!" The doctor told us he'd never heard treatment compared to a birthday party. Strides had been taken to improve side effects in the last twenty seven years!

The second day of treatment also went well. As we sat quietly in the treatment room, patients and their spouses gathering hope from one another, I wandered through the list I kept in my mind. "Home in two hours…lunch for him…nothing too spicy… nutritious…and water, lots of water, but not too much. Don't want a fluid overload….he's getting fluids now…to counteract the nausea… Oh Dear Lord, no nausea please…and supper… the roast will be for supper…oh yeah, easy on the caffeine… and laundry… where am I on that? The yard…it's okay; weed a flower bed or two… Oh it's raining… and the meds to pick up…remember to ask the blonde nurse…what is her name?? Did I get all the prescriptions? I wrote all that down in this little tablet somewhere…why can't I remember where I put things? The nurse said chemo brain was not reserved for the patient. She said I needed to rest. I did. Last night. For now, these were the things in life that I must call important…mostly making sure he was cared for.

Outside in the real world, cars were zooming by, planes were flying overhead, all filled with people going about life, most of them doing things on their own priority lists. Do we stop to think someone is sitting in a room filled with people fighting for their lives? Since our experience with cancer, I often say a little prayer when I pass a hospital or treatment center. I don't want to be driving to the spa and never consider others who may be going through a tough time. Life is made up of tough days and spa days. Any one of these people in this room would love a spa day! I looked around. Nope. Most of these folks in here just want a good day of fishing. I'll take the spa day when these treatment days are over. Suddenly the sun came out, and everything was right with the world, at least for that bright and shiny moment. I wondered if the grass would be too wet to mow today.

As we neared the end of the week, we counted the hours until it was time to go to the oncologist for the disconnection of the adriamycin. It would be a party to have it removed. It had been our constant companion for three days, a thymoma murdering machine sleeping between us at night, making its eerie sound. We anxiously waited for it to emit the beeping sound indicating it was finished and needed a rest from its part in the murder plot. It was like watching for a pot of water to boil. Where was my sword?

It beeped! Finally! We jumped in the car and drove over to Southern Hills to the doctor's office, ready for this thing to be disconnected. We believed this treatment and God were working to remove this cancer. We were visualizing victory! We expected the cancer to be gone!

"We continue to be thankful for the many prayers. We are sure that people are praying audaciously and depending on God to answer favorably. God will work the way He knows best for us. He knows me. We have met during dark and stormy times in deep valleys. We have spent time together on mountain tops. He remembers times when I've been so low in spirit I thought I'd never rise up again, and didn't care if I didn't. He made me get up. He knows when I've asked Him to perform feats on my time. He made me wait for His time. He hears me pray like a selfish whiner, all to get my way. He lets me know His way is better. I'm not His only child. He must nod in amusement when He hears me ask for the same

things over and over. Till I know a better way to pray, I'll just keep praying over and over. And... I will always pray big.

I also know I may not get my way. I know Jim may not live through this. People sometimes die. I realize that. I wish everyone could be healed and live healthy lives, but this is the world. We live in it and we see things happen we abhor. We hurt when those we love do not survive cancer. Cancer patients and their families fight hard. At the end of the battle, win or lose, we still don't have any answers. Eloquent words are not needed. They wouldn't fit anyway. No one has answers, because there are none.

There are adjustments when you finish treatment and are easing back into daily life without cancer. There is no instant turnaround. There is a kind of grief to be handled. There are those days of adjustment. When we go through cancer and come out on the other side, we are not the same as we were before. Cancer does something to you... forever."

While in the treatment room for disconnection, we old warriors encouraged new patients. The conversation continued on, patients cheering on other patients. Spouses, with tears welling up, realized that today, at least for these few moments, they didn't have to be their patient's only cheerleader. I gazed out the window to the sky. My eyes became fixed on the dark clouds looming off in the distance. From the second floor we had a front row seat view to the impending storm. The clouds stilled themselves as if waiting for some spectacular event. An electrifying bolt of lightening and a deafening clap of thunder made us all jump. We were quiet for a moment, sitting in awe, thinking maybe God was delivering His own jolt to the cancer we collectively and individually fought that day. Whether He did or He didn't, it was a good visual aid. We all knew God could hear us, and to have His storm interrupt our conversation in that particular way was a colossal moment of unity. We were strangers, yet comrades, fighting an invisible beast together with God's help.

の ら

Jim must have felt terrible as we drove home, because he didn't complain about my driving. We were beginning the not so good days. They wouldn't be permanent. We knew there would be about a ten day cycle where the same things occur. We knew these patterns and had learned by experience what would follow. We knew the ups and downs.

May 16, 2009: *"We continue to be thankful these treatments have been relatively easy. He hasn't yet experienced any nausea, but does have some fluid from the treatments. The meds are doing their job. He will have eighteen days until the second treatment begins. He will feel a bit stronger each day. He will begin rehab at Baptist to improve his lung function. Soon it will be time to set up the appointments at M.D. Anderson. We will know the effects of the chemotherapy on the tumor after two rounds.*

Today is Jim's birthday and he's having a good day. We are enjoying the quiet. It's a rainy day and a perfect day to stay inside. In the next few days counts could become low. We've learned how the chemotherapy affects his body. He may need to stay home with the germs he is used to hanging out with. He will soon be able to go about his normal activities."

May 18, 2009 "Jim hasn't felt well today. He woke up with a slight nauseated feeling. I gave him one of his anti-nausea pills, only the second one he has had to take during treatment. It makes him sleepy, but the nausea subsides. We like drowsy better than nausea. He has eaten very lightly today. I offer small snacks several times a day. Eating is of paramount importance during treatment. I don't want him to be too drowsy, so I will split the nausea pill. If that checks the nausea and leaves him less drowsy, we will both feel better. When he is drowsy, I feel the need to stay inside. I need to be outside getting the yard work done, but I don't want him to get out of his chair and fall. Being a caregiver is like juggling.

I am told that much of the nausea he feels comes from the subconscious memory of it from 1982. It works on you mentally as well as physically. I still have frightening flashbacks from those times. When he coughs a lot, it sends me right back to the time of hearing him throw up for three days. It is more than I can bear to think of it. I want him to be well again.

We were able to walk outside by late afternoon. I put a large umbrella over his sitting area. We had coffee, but the sitting didn't last long. He needed to go back inside to the comfy chair. He aches all over and stays very cold. I pray constantly for the chemotherapy to kill the cancer and spare my husband.

Tomorrow is an appointment with his oncologist for lab work. I will be able to gauge how he feels by his level of appreciation of my driving. I've almost learned the location of every bump in the road between here and Southern

Hills Hospital. He thinks I've hit most of them. I have not. He winces in pain for the car, not for himself, when hit the slightest bump. I reminded him of Steve McQueen's mustang chase in the movie "Bullitt." Did he dodge bumps in the road? He didn't even tear the car up when he hit the ground after being airborne! Jim just shook his head and said,

"That's the movies, Baby. No telling how many mustangs they tore up." Oh, really? That is why the commercials tell us not to attempt those stunts at home. I will be glad when he feels like driving again.

CHAPTER 11

Life at Home, as Love Grows

May 29, 2009 *"He will feel better when his garden is growing. He enjoys the garden spot and all that it yields. He loves seeing the first sprouts of green peek out of the ground and the excitement of seeing it grow day by day. He is absolutely in heaven when he is picking vegetables. In the fall he plants enough turnip greens to feed a small city. I may have to be the planter of this thing this year, but I don't trust my skills with a real garden. We've already asked a few people we thought might want to have a garden, but no one is up to the challenge. I am starting to feel like the little red hen."*

One morning, Jim's nephew Walter, the husband of niece Kathy, stopped by.

"I'm here to see when I can plant Jim's garden." Walter announced.

"You don't have to do that." Jim said, thinking it was a big imposition. It's a huge job and we'd already figured out that no one wanted it.

"I know I don't *have* to," Walter said, "I *want* to. When would be a good time to start?"

I could tell Walter was serious, and told him he could start whenever he'd like. He said he'd be back later in the day. What a wonderfully precious thing for Walter to do for Jim! It would be sad for Jim to see a mess of weeds growing instead of a garden. Walter Jarrell became our hero that day! Many times, through the growing season, Walter and Kathy would stop by for a visit and to check out the garden. Who could ask for better encouragers? I don't know of any gardener who doesn't love to sit down and talk about gardening. We always looked forward to their visits. Between the gardening friends and the fishing buddies, we were hardly ever without good visitors and spirited conversation. Neighbor and friend, Fred Williams is a gardener and a fisherman. He is one of our most treasured friends, neighbors and visitors!

I learned something valuable from Walter and the garden planting. In order to help Jim, it was best to show up and get to work, rather than just talk about the sad fact that the poor sick man wouldn't be able to plant his garden. If Walter had called and asked us if there was anything he could do for us, we'd have told him we didn't need a thing. Walter knew what Jim needed and he did it.

At Jim's doctor's appointment that week the test results showed why he had begun to feel terrible His white counts were lower than usual. He'd be taking an antibiotic for a little while now for precautionary measures. During this time we'd find that we needed to stay out of crowds again. As the days went by, the nausea we'd been fighting had subsided. We didn't have to use the nausea meds. Dr. McKay thought Jim looked well for what he has been through. He indicated that this chemotherapy is no small dose and he expected to see some rough days. He told us better days were ahead.

Jim drove his truck to the next doctor's appointment. He was feeling better. We were afraid his truck might not even run. No one had driven it in weeks. A spider had constructed a little web from the mirror to the edge of the carport. I didn't like the idea of Jim's truck being commandeered by spiders. It was nice to see Jim able to drive.

This appointment was with a lung specialist. All the doctors were working together to make sure Jim would have lung capacity to withstand surgery if that became part of the treatment plan. As we sat in the waiting room, I looked at our calendar for the month of May. It was only the twenty first and we had already had twelve doctor's appointments.

Jim had been retaining some fluid and had gained twenty pounds. He was up to 196 water-logged pounds. That was more than he needed to weigh, but soon it would be time for another treatment and it would dissipate by then. He was eating and sleeping well. My job was to build him up as much as possible by food and rest before the next treatment.

Walter had put the finishing touches on the garden planting. Jim's and Walter's conversation involved the fabulous quality of the soil. Only a gardener would get excited about the rolling rows of deep brown furrows, each carrying a secret known only by the gardener and The Creator. I am glad I didn't have to plant it, for it would have been embarrassing. These guys love to grow their gardens and share the bounty with others. There is a deep-seated joy of watching something grow. It is seeing God's love in action. That garden will produce not only delicious vegetables, but untold hours of enjoyment for Jim as he watches it grow. I believe he will be working in that garden before long. It gives him strength just looking at it.

According to the lung specialist's assessment, Jim is doing well for a one-lung guy who probably has some damage to his heart from radiation in 1982. His oxygen level is great. He doesn't need oxygen therapy. His breathing tests were good.

My questions for the doctor were, "Will rehab bring up his lung function? Will the frustration of almost daily appointments be outweighed by dramatic results? Would it be just as well for us to walk at the mall on days he feels like walking? How about if I work with him on exercises in the pool? Those things will keep his heart and lung from regressing. Good for physical and mental."

The doctor lit up!

"Yes, to all the exercise." The mall walking, as soon as his white counts are in a good place, would be great. He'd be in a climate controlled environment and could go during a low crowd time. That would be a perfect cardio pulmonary activity and then we can consider rehab at a later time."

"Tell him he has to do whatever I say when it comes to exercise," I added, thinking Jim would say he didn't want to go walking.

"I think he knows that."

"Yeah, I do," Jim said, getting teary-eyed. "She's the reason I'm…"

The doctor finished Jim's statement.

"Here? Yeah, she's the reason you're still on this planet."

We left the doctor's office that day with a new attitude, a new purpose and maybe a new lease on life. It seemed good. He had begun to lose the excess fluid and was eating well, knowing he needed to build his body up every ounce before the next treatment. We'd been staying outside more these days. He enjoyed sitting under the umbrella as I planted flowers in the boxes where his friends would sit when they came to visit him.

"LIFE IS....

A heartbeat
A pulse rate
A body temperature
A muscle reflex
Life is a symphony of vital organs striking chords in time...
Living is so much more."

Those were my thoughts on July 2, 1982, but they echoed in my mind this day. We continued to pray for him to get well.

છે ✦

Our goods days continued! We got up early one morning and had breakfast on the patio. It was warm, and we had beautiful sunshine. His energy level was improving. His appetite was good. I try to serve his meals in different locations and encourage him to be outside on days like this. Our pool was open now and provided a restful place to sit. There is something calming about sitting beside the water.

Kristy came over to cut her dad's hair. I asked her if it showed signs of falling out. She said it had a different texture, but it wasn't yet to the falling out stage. She said it was longer and wavier than usual, and the man just needed a good trim. He looked good, handsome.

We have handsome in this family and we have brave. Corbin, our grandson is both. He took the first swim in the seventy two degree cold water. It takes a few days for the sun to warm 22,000 gallons of water. Corbin took the title of "Bravest in the family." Mallory used to hold that record, but she gladly gave it up to little brother. We are all okay with Corbin having that title forever. No one wants in that water until it gets warmer.

Jim taught Corbin to ride a bike. He taught that lesson in about four minutes. Now we have another record! Jim has taught all of our children and grandchildren to ride a bike. We heard Jim ask Corbin if he was ready to learn to ride the bike without the training wheels. We heard Corbin's excited YES and in less than five minutes the little guy was speeding past us. He was grinning so big you could see the grin from the back of his head. He rode off across our yard and into the yard next door, a perfect down hill course! He rode and rode and rode that little bike all over the yard. What a fun day!

On days like that, we didn't think about cancer. The interaction with family and friends did so much for Jim. We tried to keep up our regular schedule of what we normally do. If Jim felt like running the weed eater or going fishing, he would do it. One of the doctors told him he should do whatever he felt like doing, and if he got tired, rest. Going about life as we knew it was best for us. That is what made for good days.

On our not-so-good days, cancer would be on our minds. On those days, there was me and God. I relied on Him. I made it, with His help, out of the dark places. He provided a way. He provided coping skills. He provided the avenue of prayer and listened and cared like no one on this earth. God knows our strengths and will help us build on them. He will hang onto us when we are weak and when the way is uncertain. He will not criticize us for our weakness, but He will take our hand when we reach for it. He will sustain us through the storms of life and we will be better for it when the storm has passed. It is during the storms we grow.

Just before the next course of chemotherapy Jim's counts began to improve slightly. We stayed home most of the week before treatment to allow him to rest and stay away from germs. In doing this, we hoped by treatment time his body would be stronger and he would have built up some resistance to infection. When his thymus gland was removed, his immune system became forever compromised. We did everything within our earthly power to help him gain physical and emotional strength so the treatments wouldn't weaken him so drastically. We were becoming familiar with the ebb and flow of good days and bad days. There seemed to be a rhythm to it. We made the best of it.

May 28, 2009: *"I believe we had a pie eating contest here last night. There was a lot of pie, much discussion of the berries for the pie, some judging of the berries in the pie, and at the end there was no pie. I think Jim's sister, Ramona won the pie making contest. It is for sure his brother; Charlie won the pie eating contest. There were no prizes, just a fun visit, lots of laughter and empty plates. We hope there will always be pies, contests, and togetherness like this."*

Jim felt good for the next few days. It must have been the pie. We did notice that his pie eating skills were up to date. He felt well enough to check out his fishing skills. He was up early making coffee and talking about fishing with his brother in law, Sonny. It wasn't long before they were in the garage preparing to transport the ship to the lake. Even though bad weather was in the forecast, they would fish until it stormed. Their plan came together. We had become well acquainted with storms.

We had been wondering when he would begin to lose his hair. A couple of weeks ago the doctor told us it would begin to fall out in a couple of weeks. That time had drawn near. We decided on a buzz cut before his hair began to fall out. When Kristy arrived to give Jim his new hairstyle, the three of us went downstairs to the cutting area. Jim sat down in the chair. Kristy put the cape around him.

Jim said, "One of us will probably cry, but it won't be me."

"I'm not crying." I said.

"Me neither! Kristy said, "I already cried all the way over here."

So, nobody cried. It is hair. It grows back. We agreed that this time wasn't as sad as in 1982, in our other cancer life. At that time we weren't prepared. This time we would be fine. Jim's hair took its regular course of leaving and was completely gone in a few days. It stayed gone for a while, but life went on. He still looked cute.

May 30, 2009: *"Friday and Saturday this week were two more good days. He is still feeling energetic. He washed his truck and even did some light gardening. He is working on a little tan on his bald head. His appetite is better than usual. During these times when he enjoys eating, we have to make the most of it. The times when he has no appetite, it seems like we are losing ground."*

We will never forget Lynn Wright's banana pudding pie! It is one of the most delicious pies we've ever eaten! Lynn called one afternoon to tell us he was bringing a pie and for us to put on the coffee. After Lynn left, the pie was sitting in the kitchen.

Jim said, "That pie is pretty enough for a picture." I took a picture of it before we started the second round of the pie eating contest. Ronnie came by that afternoon and Jim shared the pie. I decided I'd better have pie, or I'd never see it again. That had been a good decision, looked like it was time to wash and return Emily's pie plate. We never found out who told Ronnie about the pie.

Later that afternoon, we heard a little tap on the back door. Friendly people carrying food can always come in! It was Lori, Jim's niece and her daughters, Abby and Maggie. They brought us a beautiful grilled chicken salad with their delicious sweet French dressing on the side.

June 2, 2009: *"One of my highest points is when friends take time to prepare food for us. Nutrition is one of the most important parts of getting well, and the idea of friends coming by is good medicine. Friends don't have to come bearing gifts of food, but we've never turned anyone away or told them to take a pie back home! My mom and brother even delivered food from Manchester!"*

"Today, June 2, 2009, is the twenty-seventh anniversary of Jim's surgery in Houston. It was the day his right lung was removed. Every year we have thanked God for those years, months and days. And now the dreaded monster is back! I have placed this entire cancer recurrence into God's hands and I will stay focused on doing everything I can to move effectively through this time. Each day is a conscious effort to be sure no stress enters our home. Cancer is stress enough. Cancer is here every morning when we wake and it is here at

night when we go to sleep. It hangs around us every day, but we are stronger than cancer. A cancer cell by itself isn't scary. It has to multiply and make a monster out of itself before it becomes frightening. In most cases it is a fairly large creature before it is discovered. That is why we have armed ourselves with all the positive things of life: love, plenty of rest, good food and most of all, prayers that don't stop."

As I looked back over the journals I kept during the 1980's, the life I had written about was becoming all too familiar again. I was once again the caregiver, a soldier in the battle of cancer. I had become that woman again. But this time I was a better version of her. This time I was stronger, better armed with information, and much older. I was more experienced with life. I was able, with the help of God, to make it from morning to night with grace and dignity throughout this new battle. I would pray for whatever it took for us to make it through this time. I knew God would provide what we needed to make it. This was a faith builder for my children and grandchildren. Some life lessons just aren't as fun as others, but the lessons are all worth learning. You never know when some of that wisdom will come in handy. I learned a long time ago not to pray for patience. I don't like what I have to go through to gain patience. I pray instead for wisdom, tolerance, understanding and peace, and then do what it takes to grow in each of them.

A LESSON FROM THE HAMMOCK

It was a beautiful sunny Sunday afternoon! Jim and I sat outside for a while, even walked down to his garden. We enjoyed a visit with his sister Helen and her husband Jerry. They brought vegetables from their garden. Jim noticed their green beans don't come out of their garden like ours do. Theirs come out of the garden washed, broken and ready to cook. Imagine that!

After their visit I decided I'd relax a while in the hammock beside the pool. I think a nap in a hammock should be a requirement for everyone. First of all, you have to get into it. That takes a bit of effort. Then you have to give into it, trust it. Once you are into it, and you trust it for support, you will begin to lose yourself. It will hold you up totally and completely. Trust will come once you are able to turn loose of the edges with the death grip of fear. You may fill a need to grasp something familiar should you begin to fall to the ground. Once you turn loose of all things familiar, your stress will subside. Your body isn't tense. Soon your mind follows along and you are in a state of total relaxation. You begin to feel a kind of peace that isn't self designed. The only way to be at total peace in a hammock is when we are looking up toward the sky. And so it is with life. We feel peace when we look up. God's love is like a giant hammock. It supports us if we just let go. Only then can we relax in His magnificent grace and trust, knowing He realizes our needs this moment, tomorrow and forever. We only have to be willing to get into the hammock!

WABBITS

Jim had had two really good days. He was working in his garden like a real farmer. He even had the straw hat. Walter continued to stop by to lend a hand if Jim needed him. As he and Walter looked over the garden, they most likely had a discussion about the foraging rabbits. Those little critters had successfully munched up several of the young and tender squash plants. We seemed to have generations of rabbits who saw our garden as an all you can eat diner. Since bunnies are known for their large families, we may have been fighting a losing battle by trying to discourage them. Jim, as always, had a plan. I was no help. I merely thought of the stories of Peter Rabbit I'd read as a child. Rabbits have to eat too. I felt a bit guilty about seeing Jim as the mean ole Farmer McGregor, straw hat and all.

One morning at six thirty I awoke to find that Jim wasn't in the house. The security system indicated an open door. It was the garage door. I went to the garage. Jim wasn't there. I peered out every window and could not see him anywhere. His cell phone wasn't on the dresser. Fearing that he might have gone outside and fallen, I called it. He answered on the first ring.

"Hellooooo Baby." His voice was Big Bopper again.

"Where are you?" I asked. There was a brief silence. Somehow I knew he was grinning.

"I'm sittin' down here by the garden gate with my BB gun, huntin' wabbits. I've got my coffee and the paper."

"Yeah? Have you scared off any wabbits?" I asked.

"Yeah, just one. But he heard the newspaper rattling and ran off to the neighbor's garden, and I guess they see the gun."

"Really, you think they know you're after them? They notice the gun?"

"Well, yeah. They've seen this gun before."

"Ok, Elmer Fudd, I'll check ya later."

We hung up. I didn't want the rabbits to think we were conspiring against them. I hoped the neighbors hadn't seen him out there with a weapon. How could they know it was an ancient BB gun with a bad aim?

STRAWBERRIES AND DIRT

Curious things go on around here, sometimes so curious that they are actually quite entertaining. Rhonda came over one day, and brought chocolate covered strawberries. We decided to sit beside the pool and eat some (okay, all) of them. Jim said he'd take just one. He told us he was going over to Ronnie's to get a little bit of dirt. Men just love dirt. I can't tell you the number of times our lawn has been flawless. I'd be smiling as I cut the grass, totally charmed by the smooth green beauty of it all. Without warning, Jim would appear with a shovel slinging little brown shovels full of dirt over the holes. How did he know there were holes, since I was the one riding the mower all over the lawn? If he saw a squirrel dig up a nut, he'd jam the hole full of dirt. I wondered where he would put this aforementioned dirt and how much of it he would be 'putting'. All the same, I was happy that he felt like hauling dirt. Rhonda and I were having a chocolate covered strawberry kind of day.

About an hour later, Jim drove in with an entire truck load of dirt. He was ready for us to shovel it. He actually expected us to put down chocolate-covered strawberries and pick up shovels to spread dirt. The looks on our faces should have told him we had absolutely no interest in his dirt. I told him I'd be happy to shovel it the next day. I wasn't excited about the dirt project anyway. He went inside to change into dirt moving clothes. I did not see a dirt job on his to do list, but what kind of wife would I be if I let the sick man move dirt as I sat here eating strawberries? I asked Rhonda for guidance.

"I just brought the strawberries," she said. "Dad provided the dirt. I am leaving now." Nobody wanted to shovel dirt. It was a truck load! I was thinking it would be a small three shovels full. The bed of the truck was full of the stuff.

And then Sonny came by. Poor unsuspecting, kind and loving Sonny! The guy is too nice. He said he'd help spread the dirt. He was not wearing dirt hauling attire. He had been to a church meeting. We told him we could spread the dirt. Of course, by this time, I was wearing my best dirt hauling clothes. Sonny insisted that he came over especially to spread dirt. This dirt slinging job was not going to be easy. Sonny could have left. He didn't.

The three of us set out on Jim's dirt detail. It was beginning to get dark. I knew where all the tiny holes were. They were barely visible. I hoped to get the dirt poked down in the holes far enough that there weren't brown piles of it all over. Jim was driving the truck through the yard, stopping at each hole he could find. I asked him to hold the light while I shoveled. From time to time I'd find the light in my hand and Jim would be shoveling. I called a little meeting. I gave Jim the job of driving, Sonny holding the light, and I would shovel. The last thing we needed was for Sonny to injure his back again or for Jim to not be able to breathe ever again! They paid no attention to my little work plan. Somehow, the three of us took turns flinging dirt all over this property. We worked by moonlight, streetlight, flashlight and truck lights. Each time Jim would move the truck, there was Sonny with his dark tanned summer skin, sitting up on the edge of the truck bed, his church meeting shirt and pants filthy! I wondered if I should spray him down with spray and wash before he went home. I wished others could have seen us that night, but then again, no. We laughed almost as much as we flung dirt.

By ten thirty that night Sonny was sweeping out the truck bed. This job was done. People drove by slowly for the next few days. They were trying not to be obvious as they peered around the yard. I am sure they were wondering about the huge brown dots, and hoping that the same yard ailment didn't befall their yards. Not a chance. The dirt was all gone.

We make an attempt to find normal in every day. Jim and I have always enjoyed working together. The dirt job was pretty normal for us. We were happy to have Sonny along too. He lightened the dirt load, and eased the burden for us and helped turn a normal day into exceptional.

CHAPTER 12

Nothing to See Here

June 18, 2009: "We've been to the doctor today for lab work. Jim's blood work showed low numbers after the second round of chemotherapy. We expected low. He has begun to take a stronger antibiotic and will be staying home again for a few days to avoid infection from strange germs. He is tired, but it is normal for this time in treatment. We appreciate the constant monitoring during each phase of treatment. Our doctors would never say they have all the answers, but they are good at doing what they do, or Jim would not be doing this well. They have our respect and admiration.

Jim is tired and his weight is down, but he still isn't tired enough to let the rabbits have his garden. He is on the watch from time to time. He sits beside the garden in one of those antique metal lawn chairs. Those three old chairs under the shade of the apple tree make an inviting place for gardening buddies to sit. It is not a good place for rabbits to congregate. Jim holds the BB gun. The rabbits patiently munch on the neighbor's garden just down the hill below us. From there they can't see the gun. For the next few days between rabbit watch, Jim will rest, drink plenty of fluids and continue building up what the chemotherapy tore down. We pray that the chemo packed a giant punch to the beast and that Houston's tests will confirm it.

If I told anyone we were doing just fine during this time, I would have been lying. We had been doing our best to remain calm during this storm. We prayed almost to the point we felt God must be tired of our asking. I would give the cancer diagnosis to God, but then I would take it back again. On one hand I felt helpless and on the other, victorious.

We were ready for the Houston trip. We wanted to move ahead with our life, good news or bad. We packed our clothes. We loaded the car. We went effortlessly through the familiar details. We didn't know how long we'd be gone. It didn't matter. We'd just go. We left early the morning of June 15. We knew prayers were being offered for us. Everyone was aware of the weight of this trip. We would find out if Jim would need surgery or chemotherapy, or both. As we traveled, the dark weight lifted from our hearts. We began to feel peace once again.

We arrived in Houston, checked into our familiar hotel and after a night's rest, were ready for the tests. After tests were completed, we would see the doctor the next day for results. We were hours away from knowing what the plan would be for our life."

June 18, 2009: "It was time to meet with the surgeon at M.D. Anderson. Waiting had been rough. A surgeon and a nurse practitioner entered the room to give us results. During the consultation we asked if we might see the PET scan. We wanted to see if the tumor had diminished in size. I don't know why we asked, but we had seen the prior scan, showing a chest full of cancer. The doctors in the room exchanged glances for what I took to be pity on the poor patient and his wife who actually wanted to see this gross tumor. One of the doctors spoke.

"There is nothing to see. The scan was clear. It looks a thousand percent better. It almost looks normal."

There was no cancer showing up on the scan! We prayed for this to be the result. We asked God to take it away. It is gone! There was much rejoicing in that room. There were hugs and tears of joy. The box of tissues in those exam rooms aren't just for patients and their families. Doctors use them too.

As we thanked them profusely and praised their efforts, I asked them what it was like to work hand in hand with God."

Even with the tumor not showing up on the PET scan, the doctors decided it best to continue a few more treatments. After administering one round of chemotherapy, Jim's body was too weak to continue treatment. The doctors decided to hold treatment until Jim could gain more strength, a little weight, and perhaps during that time his blood could rebuild. Another concern was heart damage. Jim's heart wasn't able to compensate because of the intense radiation and chemotherapy his body has had to withstand over the years. Jim was doing well to be alive after all his body had endured. His doctors had carefully maneuvered this man through surgery, radiation and chemotherapy, knowing when to give him a break when his body needed one. These fine physicians and God had helped us through once again. The reports showed it. We felt fortunate to have been led to the right doctors throughout our journey.

We received a copy of the reports from Houston from our last visit. As I read Dr. Fossella's words, in part, "the intense activity… no longer evident." And the surgeon's words (in part) "'…complete resolution of the disease…" Once more I confirmed my belief that God is working through these men. Jim would no longer on a pending status for surgery. There is nothing in his chest to remove. The surgeon told us to go do something for fun. Take a vacation. Go to the beach! We just wanted to go home.

Jim felt well enough to take Morgan and Corbin fishing, although the heat was intense. I understand the competition was heated as well. Morgan caught the biggest fish and Corbin caught the most fish. It was a memorable day for all of them.

Dr. McKay and the doctors from M.D. Anderson communicated at length last week regarding their positions on Jim's treatment. They were overwhelmed at the tumor's response to the two courses of chemotherapy. They saw some damage to his heart. The left ventricle functioned a bit lower than normal. Adriamycin was largely responsible for the damage. They agreed to stop adriamycin and go forward with the three day treatment of the other drugs he had been getting. His red blood cells were still low. It had been suggested he have the injection or a blood transfusion to raise those counts. He was strong enough for treatment to resume once again.

Jim's hair had begun to grow back. He now had a sort of peach fuzz hair. Kristy would keep it trimmed just right so that he wouldn't look shabby. We all thought he was cute with or without hair.

Jim finished his third round of chemo. I knew the old thymoma monster felt the punch of each treatment, and we prayed the beast would stay gone. Since treatment was over for a few weeks, it was time to stay out of crowds and away from germs for a while once again. We enjoyed entertaining our guests outside when the weather was good. We were always thrilled when our neighbors Fred and Jean come up and sit and visit.

We knew it would take ten days from treatment to feel better, even with the fluids and anti-nausea meds. I carried the mask in case we encountered a sneezer, cougher or wheezer. I would whip that bad boy out like a switchblade and get it onto Jim's face before he knew what happened. By now, he was used to it. He'd barely even flinch.

AAAHHHHH, FRIDAY NIGHT!!

"Ahhhh, it is finally Friday! Dr. McKay asked if we had planned anything fun for the weekend. He said he'd make reservations for us! Wow. This is a man who knows what his patients need! I'd say that at this point, we are fun starved. Dr. McKay made a call. We knew he had connections.

We drove downtown and let the valet park our vehicle. We felt a certain relief of tension as we handed him the keys. We strolled leisurely to the elevator. The penthouse, really? We were amazed at our spacious room on the top floor. A corner room. A breathtaking view of downtown Nashville. We familiarized ourselves with all the amenities of our room. We learned how to get music or television from the remote. We found the number to call for room service. We studied the menu and ordered dinner. How wonderful to have an entire evening of easy conversation and lots of eye contact with the one we love. We were in this little hide away and no one knew we were here! Time to relax and reflect! We let the hustle and bustle of a busy week slip past us. We were totally relaxed. We heard a knock at the door (room service, we imagined). Yep. They brought us a six pack. Huh? Well, the idea of a Friday night get away was pretty. And we did get away for a few hours.

Reservations downtown? Baptist Hospital, sixth floor, corner room with a view.

Strolling leisurely? His counts were way down and his blood pressure was low. We really couldn't have walked fast.

Valet parking? I couldn't risk losing my car. The tension was eased when we knew someone else knew where our vehicle would be.

Room service? That's how hospital food comes.

Easy conversation? How hard can a crossword puzzle be, especially with two people working on it for several hours?

Eye contact? We can't hear each other unless we are looking.

The hide away? Our kids knew where we were.

The six pack? Blood platelets. Yeah, that's what they call it, a six pack.

We returned home just before dawn. But really, home after ten hours away, and Jim feeling better??? Priceless!!''

July 21, 2009: "Jim is feeling better each day, although blood work doesn't show a significant change. Perhaps these lows will be his new normal. Right now there is one more round of treatment scheduled unless his counts are too low. He may need to have a blood transfusion before the final treatment. M.D. Anderson scheduled four rounds. The treatments are carefully measured out and four is his limit for now. After the final treatment and then ten days of regaining strength, we'll go to Houston for another PET scan.

We know two treatments knocked the cancer out. These last two, we pray, were the final blows to the beast and it stays away forever. We want our life back."

The day, Jane, the nurse practitioner, called our house Jim had been to Dr. McKay's office for a checkup. Jane asked to speak to Jim. Jim wasn't home. I sensed the urgency in her voice.

"Is he home yet?" Jane asked.

"No, he isn't. Is there a problem?" I asked, feeling myself sinking.

"Well," Jane continued. "Yes there is. Another doctor was in today and saw Jim. When he listened to his heart he detected an S3 sound, which is an indication of the onset of heart failure."

I felt weak kneed and sat down.

"Jane, is he dying? Do I need to get him back home right now?" I couldn't believe what I was hearing.

"No, we just want him to see a cardiologist today, if not today, first thing in the morning. We will set it up and call you back."

"Yes. Set it up for tomorrow. He will be there." I said.

Jane, in her patient and kind way, helped me to feel less frightened. I decided not to call him on his cell phone to tell him he had heart failure. I was afraid he'd die of a heart attack from that surprise. I had to stay calm. Jane talked me through it and after I hung up the phone, I forgot what I had been doing before that phone call. I just covered up on the couch and went to sleep.

Jane called back with the cardiologist appointment information she had set for the following day. I've heard it said that life can be turned around with one phone call. I had just learned the scary truth of that.

When Jim got home late that afternoon, I told him he had an appointment the next day with a cardiologist. I was amazed at my calmness. He was not surprised at the appointment. We normally had twenty appointments a month.

When dinner was ready, we took our food down to the patio. By this time it was early evening. The sun had left its cozy warmth inside the lower patio. I flipped the switch to the pool light and gave a soft glow to the area. I put on some music. As we ate, Jim told me about his day and then asked what I thought was up with the cardiologist, if anything.

"Jane says the doctor who listened to your heart today heard something that hasn't been there before. It is called an S3 sound and could indicate the onset of heart failure," I told him. He looked shocked. I went on to explain what I could and I told him not to be afraid. It wasn't a life or death emergency. Big brave me; I was shaking in my flip flops.

The next morning we met our cardiologist. When she walked into the room she looked shocked.

"You are Mr. Oakley?"

"Yes."

"Well, well, well, I was actually dreading this visit. Your chart Dr. McKay sent over is very thick. I knew I would never be able to read it before meeting you. I just scanned for highlights. I was afraid I would see a thin, sick man. You look remarkably well for what you've been through."

She began to explain what we would need to do. She was talking fast, quickly noting some things as she talked. She told me these were important things for me to do and that she'd give me the list once she was finished talking us through the information. It was all so new.

She pointed to a particular sentence and said, "This is most important!" She put little stars beside it and then her hand smudged the ink when she moved it.

I am always able to quickly retain and execute instructions and details, but suddenly I felt totally unable to follow the doctor's words. I was overwhelmed by the smudged ink. I suddenly felt the room spinning. I was hot and cold at the same time.

I was thinking, "That is most important. I need to take it with me and it is smudged. How will I ever read it?" She continued talking fast and writing faster.

She looked at me and asked, "Are you okay?"

"No, I don't feel well." I managed, embarrassed that she had noticed. She got up and moved toward me.

"Did you eat today?"

"I had coffee." I answered.

"Are you feeling any pain in your chest, arm or jaw?" she asked.

"No, just dizzy and my chest feels tight." I said, choking back a lump in my throat.

Jim looked at me and asked, "What's wrong?" I pushed back tears, but my eyes were blurry with the threat of them spilling over onto my cheeks.

"She never cries." He said.

"Tell you what we are going to do," the doctor said, "We have an EKG machine right outside this door. I would like to treat you to a complimentary test. It will make me feel better to know there isn't more going on with you."

"That's fine." I replied. The test was quickly done. No problems were indicated. With a normal EKG under my belt, I felt better, but I knew I wasn't okay yet. I was about to have a panic attack; however, it would have been stupid to die of a heart attack in the treatment room of a cardiologist. It's best to check those symptoms out. The doctor looked at me and then at Jim, then she spoke just to me.

"A little while ago, I saw you stifle what might have been a good cry. You need to do that. I am finished with you all for today and I don't need this room. I want you to stay in here as long as you need to and finish that cry. You can even order lunch if you want to, but don't hold back those tears."

Jim looked uneasy and we both thanked her. She left the room. I sat there for a moment, appreciating her helpful gestures toward my health, mental and physical. Jim was looking at some literature the nurse had brought in for us to take home. I felt awkward. I excused myself and went to find the car. I thought I might cry there, but I couldn't anymore. Instead I felt the breeze on my face, closed my eyes and pictured another place far, far away. I pictured an ocean, a beach, a sunny sky, just anywhere but here. And before I knew it, I had successfully pushed my feelings down once again. Cancer, we had been handling just fine. Heart failure, we didn't need. I doubted it would go away with my denial, but I didn't want to know any more about it today. I had had enough!

We came home with Jim's newly prescribed heart meds, and now our house looked like a pharmacy. Just one more indication that sick and dying people live here. We now have medicine and all the literature to go with it. All we needed was a literature rack to stand it on and categorize it. Here we have your cancer tracts, your heart failure tracts and your dietary section for heart healthy cooking. Cancer patient cooking ideas are over here, with the special emphasis upon avoiding nausea.

Over there is a whole section on avoiding salt. I didn't want all that clutter and wondered how we could hide it. Who wants to display all that medicine? It didn't take long to find a nice cabinet.

I was glad Jim had gained a great cardiologist. She was encouraging and compassionate. I was able to interpret the notes she jotted down for us. I began to read the heart health literature. It was logical and good advice. I would need to make some adjustments in the culinary department. I had to joke about it before I could let it sink into my southern fried brain.

"In this house, we do not need to read about how to eat. We have eaten before. Greasy southern fried everything is goooood. Bacon grease? Butter? Not Good? We cook with it, smear it and pour it over our food. Sometimes we wear a little of it on our shirts. We keep spray bottles of stain remover in the kitchen! We are known in this house for our fried apricot pies. Ok, I get it. I realize which foods are not for every day enjoyment. I promise to do better.

I do cook kind of heart smart, but I still have a lot to learn. With all this information at hand, I will be a whiz of a heart smart cook. I see no banana pudding pie, peach cobbler of thick crust pizza among those recipes. Grease will not exist, at least not in the portions we have been accustomed to. This will be a challenge. We will grill our vegetables instead of drowning them in bacon grease. We will be good. Our food will not be as good as it was, but we will be healthier than we were.

In September of 2009 we were operating under almost normal conditions. The last time we saw Dr. McKay his orders were for Jim to go fishing. There has been a lot of fishing and a lot of gardening. Jim had an amazing tomato crop and has planted the turnip greens. We are closing the tomato factory in our kitchen and will soon open the turnip green factory. Jim has been feeling well. His garden provides much more than food to cook and share. It gives Jim a great deal of satisfaction from planting to harvesting. It is therapy. Fishing? That is also therapy. Unless you been with him and caught a boat load of fish, you cannot appreciate it. Yeah, sometimes he takes me along!

Our September trip to Houston once again gave us good results. We are feeling so blessed. I seem to forget from one visit to the next that the scan takes about three hours from prep to finish. I always begin to pace, thinking it is taking too long. About the time I am ready to ask about him, he saunters out with a cup of water and a fishing magazine. I've been nervously straightening up the tract racks in the waiting room. He is thinking about his next fishing trip. That's the way we handle it.

Much has happened since May 2009 when this second battle with cancer began. We continue to rejoice as Jim's health and quality of life improves a little each day. The cancer is gone, and his heart is functioning well with the medicine the cardiologist prescribed.

As we look back over these last months, we have to ask ourselves,

"What just happened? Was that us?" We had tough days, but we had more good days. We're thankful to have made it to this side of the story.

Attitude plays a hug role in the trials of life. Even if the news is bad at the end of the illness and the patient doesn't get well, there are benefits from possessing a certain positive expectancy. Finding positive things each day to do is especially helpful. The things one might take for granted become positive pauses in the day. Things like a nap, a nice lunch out doors, an ice cream sundae or a banana split, a crossword puzzle shared with a friend. Those small things help to give the days a bit of unique beauty. These things are a distinct indication that you appreciate one another enough to incorporate ways to share happiness and love.

How did we make it? We don't know. We have had a lot of help from our families, friends and God. Life this way hasn't been what we would have chosen, but it has been our life, warts and all. We've gained from it. I believe we've gained more than we've lost. Our life hasn't been like anyone else's we know. We wouldn't trade it with anyone else either.

I find it exciting to hear about other people's exotic and luxurious trips. I love seeing their photos of all the places they've been. It is fun to hear of their unique and wonderful experiences. I am especially intrigued by the cruises. The photographs of the seas in faraway places are enchanting and hold a beauty only God could have created. How else could we have the beautiful blues of sea and sky intermingling in a palette of perfection? Without the beauties of nature, the journeys we take wouldn't be as meaningful.

I realize Jim and I have had our journeys too. We've seen some blue skies and some raging seas. We weren't on the actual cruise ship. The scenery we saw at times was dismal and at other times, more beautiful than words can tell. Even though there were times through our struggles with cancer when we were hanging on for dear life, we've made all our trips well.

CHAPTER 13

Rejoice! Roadtrip. Reality.

On October 17, 2009 we held a rejoice party. Fifty-five people came to our home, making for a memorable evening. Kristy and Rhonda coordinated the food. All I had to do was clean the house and set up tables. We had fabulous Mexican food spread over a twenty foot serving table. This didn't include the desserts. We had been concerned about the weather, since this was to have been an outside event. That night was the coldest night we'd had in October. The children, even thought it was freezing cold, still ran around outside playing, shedding their jackets. I cautioned them about the sixty degree pool water. After I gave the children the killer cold water speech, I heard a child's voice from across the pool say,

"We will be careful for our lives." Lesson heeded. No one got wet that night.

After dinner we lit the fire pit and the children made s'mores and chased one another around with hot pointed sticks. The Good Lord was watching over us in many ways. We had a time of prayer and thanksgiving and were drawn closer once again as we felt God's love and blessings on our lives. It was good to be gathered to rejoice. We had asked God for so much. He heard our prayers and answered them. We wanted to gather together to show Him our appreciation.

We don't know why God has answered our prayers so perfectly and in just the way we asked, but He knows. He has our attention and our hearts. That night was perfect in so many ways. It felt good to have fun again. After everyone left, Jim and I agreed that the evening went by much too quickly. It didn't matter about the cold weather outside. It was warm inside our house. It was just right. We knew God was pleased.

The rejoicing was wonderful. We knew we had been blessed. We had been given so much. Did we dare, once again, to petition God to restore Jim's health? In two months we would be going back to Houston for another checkup. The prayer requests would begin again. We hoped it would be followed by rejoicing.

Our departure day was a fine day for travel, and our little white mustang loved the gallop. I did most of the driving while Jim rested. We were leaving the cool Tennessee weather and would soon enjoy some warmer Texas air. That is one of the best parts of Texas in December. It was a perfect day for driving. Jim was sleeping. I cranked up the music and opened a package of something chocolate with a lot of calories.

By early evening the fog had begun to settle in. It had wrapped that area in the middle of nowhere in a thick slimy blanket. Driving was messy. Visibility was poor and depressing. The road had a lot of sandy gritty stuff that when mixed with wet, made for a creepy sound under the tires. The Christmas lights decorating the little few and far between homesteads made it worse. We felt suspended in time. We decided this area looked like any place deep in the south, just name the state.

By the time the Houston skyline appeared we felt we could center our minds on reality, but we were still going to a cancer center. I had not shopped nor decorated for Christmas. It was the fifteenth of December, and I really did not care. It would get done and we'd smile and act like it had all been easy.

We checked into our hotel, made popcorn, watched some television and retired early with thoughts of the next day's schedule of blood work and a CT scan dancing in our heads.

Each time we visit Houston, we meet people who don't have it so good. Not everyone gets a good report. Not everyone here is going to get out of this alive.

Dear friends of ours, Micky and Linda Bell had not gotten good reports for some time. Micky's reports went from bad to worse. We visited with them often when we'd go to Houston. There were times we could not call them when Jim's test results were good and Micky's were bad. It seemed cruel. Why would one man get well and the other not? It seemed unfair. We knew they would be happy to hear our good news, but we wanted so desperately for Micky to have good news also. Our hearts were broken as Micky's health declined. He fought cancer with all that was in him, yet he still possessed a faith and courage that was a lesson for all of us. His trust in God was beautiful and remarkable. He died on March 17, 2010.

I cannot read Second Timothy 4:7, 8 - "I have fought the good fight, I have finished the race, I have kept the faith. Now there is in store for me the crown of righteousness, which the Lord, the righteous Judge, will award to me on that day—and not only to me, but also to all who have longed for his appearing"- (NIV) without thinking of Micky Bell. Sometimes there are no words to say to friends whose loved ones have died. I believe being there for them is what we must do. Sometimes it is the only thing we can do.

December 21, 2009: *"Jim and I would like to thank everyone for your constant prayers for us this past year. We know we have never been far from your thoughts. We have felt the effects of your prayers. It means so much to know we have so many who are willing to continue to petition God on our behalf. We thank you also for joining with us to praise God and to thank Him for these answered prayers. We are humbled beyond what words can convey. We are in awe of where these last few months have taken us. We are somewhat off kilter still from where we now find ourselves. Getting well is also an adjustment. There is a mindset you have to put yourself into when you are fighting a disease that may kill you. It takes a little while to move that out of the way and cope with everyday life after chemotherapy and doctor's appointments. It has been a wild rollercoaster ride, but for now, today, we stand on solid ground. Jim is doing well. Our most recent report shows no presence of cancer."*

We left Houston after seeing the doctor, thinking we would drive about half way, check into a hotel, find a great Italian restaurant, have dinner, then get a good night's sleep. In the morning we'd wake up refreshed to drive the few hours home. We were having a good day of driving. The weather was perfect and we didn't feel the least bit tired. Jim was driving and I was playing with the GPS.

"Hmmmm," I said, "If we drive straight through, we can be home by three am." Jim looked surprised and asked if I really wanted to do that. I mulled over the pros and cons for about three seconds and said, "Yes, I do. Drive!" He got us out of

Houston. I promised to drive after the next gasoline stop. That stop came soon and I drove for a few hours while he slept. It felt like there was just me, my music, and the big trucks out here on the road. I'd been playing this like a giant game board. Home was the prize. I liked winning. I was passing them all.

After a hamburger stop, Jim drove the last part of the trip. I guess he was tired of the little game, or he feared he was riding with a maniac. The weariest part of the trip is the last part when you are just a couple of hours from home. I would not dare to go to sleep while he was driving. I watched the road just as closely as he did until we were safe in our very own driveway. We ditched the car and everything in it for the warmth of home. It was just a little after three am. We were anxious to put Houston behind us for three or four months. It was time to think about Christmas.

The four months between trips are usually bearable at home. We go through each day and before we know, the whole week has passed by. We stay involved with all the activities of our life. We don't dwell on cancer. We try to be positive. These four months were just tough ones. Winter seemed darker than usual. Spring came to our rescue, putting back the light that winter had snuffed out. We anticipated our next Texas trip with a new level of excitement. We were ready to go. These are our mini vacations. M.D.Anderson Cancer Center's landscaping is the only tropical setting we will ever see.

CHAPTER 14

Our Life on the Road

April 2010: *"The report from Houston is another good one. Jim is still cancer free. We will return in four months, sometime in August. I don't ever want to take these good reports for granted. I anticipate them. Hope keeps me sane. At the same time I know that one report at any time can show the cancer has returned. I will not dwell on the negative part of any of this. There is just no need for that. It is energy wasted."*

Our August trip to Houston proved to be another visit with good results. He had now been cancer free for a year. We have hope. Last time he was cancer free for twenty-seven years. I thank God for those twenty seven years, but I thank Him even more for this last year. I am thankful that the cancer was detected and could be treated. We would enjoy getting back to our life, once again, without cancer.

"We've spent a lot of time in a place where everyone we see is affected by cancer. While M.D. Anderson is a beautiful facility, it is still a place where a dark beast lurks in hidden places. That beast is destroying life and love and breaking hearts. I still become emotional when I see the massive M.D. Anderson Cancer Center spread over more than three hundred acres and know this place, with its talented and

dedicated specialists and God restored Jim in 1982. We've had healing again in 2010. We are indeed blessed. This is our life. We don't want to live in fear of recurrence. We are forever being watchful and never letting down our defenses. We are being stalked by a wicked thing who tries to remain invisible until it has commandeered a major organ. There is a need for fervent prayer for families affected with cancer. This is real life and sometimes it is more frightening than you can imagine."

DECEMBER 2010

I drove a lot of the way to Houston while Jim slept. He was surprised to be in Arkansas when he awoke! He was amazed that I had beaten him in the miles per gallon contest, and that he hadn't been tossed out of his seat like a crash dummy. I think he might have also been amazed that I paid attention to the gauges and didn't just look at the scenery. I know the scenery by heart. The mpg contest was a good diversion. We noticed each time we stopped, the weather was getting warmer. We left cold and snowy and liked the idea of a few days of warm and sunny. When the temperature hit seventy I thought it would be a great idea to put the top back on the car. Jim said it was not a good idea. All our junk would blow out of the back seat! I glanced back to see how bad it would be if we lost the junk. I noticed cookies. We could think about stashing the junk later. We had cookies to eat.

I don't want it to seem like we don't have moments of anxiety. We do. Before most of the doctor's appointments, Jim feels little twinges and aches he doesn't normally feel. It isn't that we don't trust God for good results but, we wonder who are we to ask and receive such good. There are others who are sick who ask earnestly and they don't get well. We have friends who have died! They believed God would heal them. I don't have the answers. I won't try to find pretty words to make it better. There are none. I do know that God, in His infinite wisdom, is in charge of the plan and the time schedule. Not us. Yes, we do have our moments. I try to keep mine to myself. I tried sharing them once or twice and was told that my faith was weak. Never let anyone tell you when you are experiencing a not-so-good day your faith is weak.

We received another good report on that December 2010 trip and were soon on the road to home and a tender Tennessee Christmas.

February 22, 2011. It was a basal cell carcinoma that went wild. We never know how a small pimple-sized, not so unusual looking lesion could go so ballistic. It just sat there on the back on Jim's neck, right under the edge of his shirt collar. Kristy noticed it while she was cutting his hair. She felt it had changed and suggested he see a dermatologist. His shirt collar could be irritating it, but, it looked different. We scheduled a doctor's visit. It was diagnosed as a basal cell carcinoma. Basal cell is the most common type of cancer. It rarely metastasizes or kills. It can destroy tissue. It is considered malignant. Most basal cells are easily treated.

After treating it a couple of times, it wasn't healing. This was about an eighteen month period of not healing. During this time I had been cleaning and dressing the area daily. I had lulled myself into believing it was healing. Some days it really did look better. After the excision, it was about the size of a bottle cap and was a sunken little crater. One day I noticed a discolored rim around it. It looked as if it were trying to heal but failing miserably. It had become glaringly obvious that this thing was continuing to grow outward, and probably inward. It was time to go back to the dermatologist. She agreed it was time for microscopic surgery. It sounded reasonable. We scheduled it. Prior to the surgery, an MRI was ordered so the surgeon could see how far this hateful thing had pushed itself into Jim's neck. With his compromised immune system, we realized his healing time would not be normal, but eighteen months of healing was certainly abnormal. The Mohs surgery seemed to offer a believable approach to removal and healing.

I was impressed with the idea of Mohs surgery. It is a surgical procedure developed in the 1930's by a general surgeon, Dr. Frederic Mohs. It is now primarily used by dermatologists as a cure for basal cell and squamous cell skin cancers. The surgery consists of deadening the vicinity of the tumor and using a dye to mark the area. The cancer is then shaved away, a little at a time and carefully examined under a microscope, testing for presence of cancer cells. The surgery continues, and can last for hours. The surgery is completed when clear margins are determined. The patient is allowed to take small breaks during the procedure. We came prepared to spend the day.

As soon as the first markings were done, I left the exam room. I had only been in the waiting room a few minutes when Jim came out to sit with me. I guessed the first part of the surgery had been done and the waiting had begun.

They called both of us back to the treatment room. We knew this wasn't a good sign. The surgical nurse motioned for Jim to go ahead to the treatment room. She touched my arm to hold me back.

"I want to get you a stool to sit on when you look at the site." She said gently, still touching my arm.

"It's much larger now." I felt a stab of pain in my chest, but considering the anxiety I was feeling, it seemed a normal reaction for this moment. I knew the site would be larger, but I expected it would be bandaged and ready for us to go home.

I promised the nurse I would be fine. I had dealt with a much larger incision than this. I had taken care of the incision when his lung was removed. I would not pass out. I didn't want to frighten Jim by being squeamish. I've seen surgical sites, more than my share. I loved this man and he depended on me to not pass out. I would be fine. When I walked into the room, Jim was sitting in the surgical chair with his head bent forward. The area was deadened. He was fine. I moved to the back of the chair with the nurse and observed the site.

"See? This is all we could do. It is just too deep." She told me. We turned our attention to the doctor.

"As I made the first incisions, I could see that it was going to be too large for me to do any good. I recommend a head and neck surgeon. Do you have any questions?"

"Yes, this *is* malignant, isn't it?" I asked.

"Yes. It is, most definitely." He replied. With this huge basal cell crater on the back of Jim's neck, we set out to begin scheduling a head and neck surgeon.

Here we were in scary world again. After meeting with his oncologist, Dr. Erter, and speaking with the Houston oncologists, it was determined that the head and neck surgeon would be the one to take his best shot at closing the large gaping hole in the back of this rather tired of being cut on neck.

The surgery was scheduled for March 2, 2011. We arrived at the hospital a bit before six am. The procedure took an hour and a half. The surgeon, a miracle worker of a man, closed the wound with an eight inch incision without having to use any type of skin graft. That's one of the perks of being kind of old. Your skin is more pliable. The doctor felt this incision would heal well. We left for home happy and smiling. We proudly carried our instructional information on caring for the post of site and would be back each week until it was healed. There have been no problems since.

The basal cell event almost put me under the rug. My energy level dropped. I fought fear and doubt. I felt the devil swoop over me like a huge mean bird. The sounds I heard inside my head were like a dark noise that chanted,

"This is it. It is over. He will die. Give up." It is the meanness only prayer can diffuse.

FOR BETTER OR WORSE

Cancer is life altering. Life is full of twists and turns and there are many reasons to think of what the phrase, for better or worse, is all about. The trip Houston went well.

We left home a little earlier than normal, hoping to arrive in Houston before dark. We tried not to stop as frequently. Neither of us had an appetite. It didn't matter. We just drove. Jim hadn't been feeling well lately. Sometimes he would develop a cough. It would get violent and wear him out. He would lose sleep. The cough would interfere with his appetite. The cough brought back desolate memories for both of us. He had been coughing for a week. There was a cough medicine that helped, but it was a narcotic. The drowsiness from the narcotic was more than we could handle. If he slept too much, he wouldn't eat. If he didn't eat, well he was thin, and he needed to eat.

He coughed all the way to Houston. I drove most of the way. He insisted on driving for a little while and we both were miserable. We made him a nest in the back seat and he slept some. I was able to scoot us along the road a little faster with him asleep. I halfway hoped a trooper would stop us. I was thinking,

"Just stop me state trooper. Look at this sick guy in the back seat. Get us to Houston. This car's odometer says it can go 160. Just lead the way." We arrived in Houston about six pm, much earlier than normal.

Coughing continued most of the night, until I finally gave him a half dose of the narcotic junk. It might be ok for him to be drowsy the next day for the scan. He absolutely could not cough during a CT scan. I was excited to learn that Jim made it through the scan and the x-ray without coughing. Our results were given the following day. The report was mostly good; however, there was some infection showing up in his chest. We were not surprised. All this coughing had to present some evidence of infection. The word cancer wasn't mentioned. Dr. Fossella gave him two prescriptions and scheduled us for July. We'd return again in four months.

Before we left Houston, the weather stations were reporting huge thunderstorms marching across the entire U.S. Our folks at home were in touch with us by phone often, giving us the progress report on the storm's location. Everyone told us to stay in Texas another night. It sounded like a good idea to me. Jim still didn't feel well. We wanted to go home, but we didn't want to be in the eye of the storm. We were already in a storm of our own, and it was big enough. We decided to leave Houston and stop for the night if we ran into the storm. It wasn't a question of *if*, more like *when*. This storm was everywhere. We started driving.

A horrid windy downpour met us in Arkansas. It hit with no warning. Driving was almost impossible. Intense amounts of water stood on the road. We got off the road at the next exit. We were more than ready to stay overnight now! Everybody on the road had the same idea. There were no vacancies anywhere.

We stopped at three hotels before we found a vacancy. Seemed everyone had the same idea. When we signed in we looked like a couple of homeless drowned rats. They took us in anyway. We were fortunate to find a room at all. We checked into their last available room. When we turned on the television we knew that stopping here had been a good decision. It was reported that the small town of Marshall, Texas, where we had stopped for gasoline a couple of hours before, had been hit hard by large hail and winds. We had considered staying in Marshall when we stopped. It's a pretty town with some new hotels and good places to eat. The sun had been shining in Marshall when we stopped. Since the weather was good, we felt like driving a while longer. We didn't know the storm was that close.

By morning the skies were clear, but storms were still raging in front of us as well as behind us. It would be a toss up as to which storm we'd be trying to dodge. We left Arkansas mid morning and by the time we reached Tennessee we could see the high water and downed trees for miles. It had been a horrific storm with too much rain for the ground to absorb. We heard the storm was on its way to middle Tennessee.

It was good to get home. Jim was sick when we left and he was sick when we got home. I felt the responsibility of driving most of the way. It began to rain hard just about an hour out of Nashville. By the time we drove into the driveway we were tired out and almost prayed out. Sleep sounded like a good idea. I couldn't shake the feeling that something just felt weird. I guessed that it was because I didn't have my normal fun travel buddy. Everything about this trip had been a bit unsettling. We would make this trip again in August. It took a while to feel rested, and we tried our best to move ahead with life as we knew it. August arrived much too soon. Jim still didn't feel well.

It was August 25, 2011 and we were traveling on my mother's birthday. I wished I was having lunch with my mother. If life were different, that is what I would be doing, but these trips were essential. They had to be scheduled in certain monthly increments in order for the doctors to track the disease. Should it recur, we don't want it to get a head start on us.

We arrived in Houston just before a rain storm hit. That felt too familiar. We had a good trip out. It rained all the way. Normally when we stop for gasoline one of us washes bugs off the car. There were no bugs. They don't stick when there is rain. We would describe this drive to Texas was like being in a fourteen hour car wash stuck on the rinse cycle.

Jim drove from Nashville to Jackson. In Jackson he announced that he was tired of driving. Funny guy. He asked me if I was ready to drive. Sure. All I needed was cool air, fifties music, coffee and for him to get his pillows, make a nest and close his eyes. He did. He got all pillowed down, blankets on and a jacket over his head. It looked like I was transporting elephant man down the interstate. We traveled like that through Arkansas until we stopped for fuel. He had slept the entire time. We made it to the hotel by eight thirty that night. The next morning we both felt refreshed and ready for our day.

Our hospital routine was familiar. It was quiet and peaceful. It isn't so much like a hospital visit, well unless you are the one behind the doors, beyond the designer carpets, fountains and sculptures. Back there is where they keep the needles and where they do the testing and the treatments. Out here we pray for the ones who have to be back there. We bide our time and we pace and we pray. We try to keep our wits about us as the rest of the world goes by.

CHAPTER 15

Fighting Another Round

We knew something wasn't right as we were waiting for results. The nurse came out twice to say the CT scan report wasn't ready. Since we were planning to leave for home after this appointment, we decided to use this time to go have lunch. Waiting was normal, but we both felt a little foreboding as we waited. We had been waiting three hours when the doctor came in with results. He told us the cancer had returned. This was the third time for this thymoma monster. I felt devastated. Jim handled the news well. Jim and I are never devastated at the same time. We began our trip home in silence. I did not want to make phone calls. The one call I most needed to make would be the one to Dr. Erter's office in Nashville to schedule chemotherapy once again. Our children are always first on the list. We need to know that they have the correct information before the phone calls begin. That is one reason I am glad to use the internet. I can say it one time and information can be received by many. My message that day was simple and succinct.

August 27, 2011 *"Thank you for your prayers. I have signed in several times to give you an update. I simply could not find any words. We didn't get the good report we had hoped for.*

The cancer has returned. It is in the right chest wall again. Jim will begin chemotherapy as soon as possible. The oncologists have set up a plan of action. We will go back to Houston for scans during the course of the treatment and continue to be monitored by both teams. We continue to ask for your prayers as we go into battle against this monster again."

The cancer is usually slow growing, lazy, but mean. It is confined to the lower right chest where the lung was removed in 1982. It is probably fairly early in the growth cycle of these cancerous nodes. The same drugs will be used which have shown to be effective against a malignant thymoma. This treatment won't be as aggressive, but both doctors believe it will be a good option. We can't use adriamyacin any longer. It is the drug that attacked and killed the thymoma, but it damaged Jim's heart in the process. We cannot risk further heart damage.

Jim's treatment was scheduled to begin on September 6, 2011 for this, the third fight with the thymoma beast. We went in for the treatment to begin. He was signing forms and the nurse was asking him the routine questions. She asked him if he had had any chest pains. He had and was not going to mention them. My common sense told me that the chest pains he had the night before needed to be mentioned. We'd come this far and the last thing we needed was for him to go into cardiac arrest. He was sent to the cardiologist for an EKG. She saw no immediate danger and cleared him for treatment.

Jim seemed to do well during the course of treatment. He continued feeling well. He said he would like for people around him to go on as they normally do. He felt like working his part time job with the car dealerships. He went fishing a couple of times and also played cards with his buddies: Fred Williams,

Sonny Gossett, Jim Hall, Carlos Denny, Joe Paty, Jerry Carver and his brother Ronnie. In accordance with his request for everyone to go about life as they normally do, I made a small list of things around the house for him to do. He came in one night after playing cards, picked up the list, read through it and put it back on the table. Life was pretty normal.

By the fourth treatment Jim began to feel tired and experienced some slight nausea. His blood work was low, but not low enough to hold treatments. The next scheduled trip to Houston showed that the treatment is working. It was a good report to hear. We did not ask any questions. When Dr. Fossella said, "We are pleased with the results." That was good enough for us. The tumor had not grown.

By the end of January we felt we were on overload. Jim had had his seventh treatment. He began to experience some breathing difficulties. We were in that window of time when he is prone to have lower numbers in his blood work. It seems to go along with the treatment. This time was a bit worse. Jim has done quite well tolerating the chemo. These drugs are toxins. They kill the cancer and they cause problems in other ways. His doctors carefully monitor his progress. We thank God for their abilities and their caring spirits. We know we have to pay particular attention to how his heart is functioning.

On one particular morning Jim felt terrible when he got up. He had coughed during the night, but nothing that caused either of us to be alarmed. It was just sort of an irritating cough that he felt he needed to do. It sounded like a fake cough.

A couple of times he said, "Really, I don't know why I am coughing. I just cough." We laughed it off, but the coughing became more frequent. I called the oncologist's office just before noon to ask if we could come by and let them listen to his chest. He had finished his treatment a few days before and had taken his final meds as directed. He was coughing more as the day went by. By the time we reached the doctor's office, his every breath was a cough. It was wearing him out. I was afraid he'd die on the way to the office! The doctor listened to his chest and immediately hooked him up to an IV with lasix. He was drowning! Dr. Erter gave us two choices: Extra lasix and go home, or admit him to the hospital and continue the IV lasix. I did not want to take him home only to bring him back to the ER later. Dr Erter agreed. He'd probably be coming back. This was serious. He was admitted quickly.

The next day he was moved to the critical care unit, not because he was critical, but because he could be monitored more closely with the pulmonary staff right outside his door. A guy with one lung and heart damage needed to be in direct proximity to the emergency care, should he need it. We felt better with him in the hospital.

Before I left him that night, I tucked him in with extra pillows and blankets and turned off the lights. They would let him sleep until it was time for a breathing treatment. He was being observed through his little glass room.

As I was leaving his hospital room that night, he thanked me again for taking such good care of him and then said, "There is no one in this world that can do what all you do. Super Woman, go home and sleep."

And so I did.

I slept until I got a call from our daughter in law, Crystal. She was calling to tell me that Greg, our son, had been admitted to the hospital in Paris, Tennessee after a near death emergency.

He had lost most of the blood in his body from a GI tract bleed. He received six units of blood. He had driven home from work in an extremely weakened condition where he later collapsed and had to be taken to the hospital by his wife and other family members. They had agreed it wouldn't be wise to wait on the ambulance. Crystal assured me that everything was being done for Greg to help him get better. I could not let my mind wander to the place where I thought what would have happened if Crystal had not been there. My precious son could have died. My heart was being ripped out. I knew Crystal would be right by Greg's side and make sure he was receiving the care he needed. She possessed the strength and the tenacity it would take to see him through this.

Jim was feeling better the next morning when I went to the hospital to sit with him. I needed tell him about Greg. We were unable to leave this hospital and go see our son; however, our being with him would not have helped him to get well any sooner. It was a time when patience and trust in God had to take over our tender feelings. We felt assured he was receiving the care he needed and would stay in touch with Crystal. I knew I would be going to go see Greg if I had to hire a babysitter to stay with Jim!

Jim said, "Crystal is like you. She will be able to handle this. She will be sure he gets the right care. He will get well again." I agreed. Several of the Oakley women were wearing super woman capes right now. We were all being strong for each other, and for our men.

At the same time, Jim's brother Ronnie was in the hospital having a brain biopsy. He had three lesions on his brain. He had renal cancer a few years before. It had recently metastasized to his brain. Ronnie did not know Jim or Greg was in the hospital. It was evident Ronnie noticed Jim's absence. We sent him word that Jim was coughing and shouldn't be visiting in the hospital. It was exactly the truth. He was coughing. He shouldn't be visiting in the hospital. He needed to be a patient in the hospital. When Jim's coughing subsided, he was able to give Ronnie a brief phone call. We hoped that phone call would relieve Ronnie of the feeling something wasn't quite right. He was not a guy you could trick. Even with his reduced capacity to speak, he could still think, see and hear. He would scan every face in the room for clues as to what was going on.

It was several days before Jim was able to breathe without the aid of oxygen. His fluid overload crisis was past. He was still coughing and continued having breathing treatments. His sense of humor was returning, which is always lets us know he feels better. I didn't want to bring him home until his chest was quiet. I saw one of the doctors and asked about the results of the CT scan. He told me the results were in and they looked good.

He said, "There is something that looks like calcification in the chest wall."

"We don't do *looks like*, is there something else we need to do?" I asked.

He said, "We could look at the last scan results from M.D. Anderson and compare, but you'll need to sign for it." I told him to get me a pen.

We didn't come this far to settle for what something looks like. This cancer is aggressive and cruel. It doesn't care who it kills. I will spend the rest of my days making sure that it isn't sneaking up on us. If it leaves any clues, I will find them. This cancer has been our enemy since 1982. I still have some fight left in me and I will battle it to the death. Jim is doing his part. I am doing mine.

My daughter Kristy, granddaughter Mallory and I finally got to go to Paris, Tennessee that weekend to see Greg. Rhonda was happy to uncle-sit for the day. Crystal had been at the hospital with Greg the entire time. He seemed to be feeling much better. He was preparing for another test for the following day. They were ready to do surgery if they needed to in order to correct the bleed. We knew God was taking care of all of our patients. Crystal seemed confident that the right things were being done for Greg.

To think that my precious son could have died just broke my heart. I knew God won't put more on us than we can handle, but this Lord, this was a mountain. I knew He would give us the strength to climb, but I was already so weary from climbing. I wondered if the Lord could give us a nice sandy beach instead. Just for a little while. I found myself telling God to take me, take my husband, but don't take my children!

Each day that week we had prayed for the next day to be better. We thanked God each day that we made it through. Jim, Ronnie and Greg all belonged to God. We wanted to keep them. We wanted them to be well. It was getting to be too much to sort through. I found myself praying collectively, individually and other times just staring blankly into space looking to the sky saying, "What Lord? What?"

If not for my daughter, granddaughters and my daughter-in-law, I would not have been able to cope my way through those days. I sometimes wondered if God was tired of listening to me.

It was comforting on Sunday to have our congregation made aware the Oakley family was in crisis. A special prayer on our family's behalf was prayed. Many times we just sit there in church with so much pain. We dare not bring our pain to anyone's attention, lest they think we are weak. We *are* weak! We don't have any strength at all without Jesus. When we think we can stand on our own, we just fall flat. I felt the effects of those prayers that day from the people in our congregation. I had entered that building with anxiety overload. I left with the knowledge that I was not alone in these days of crisis.

Jim was released from the hospital after a little over a week. Dr. Erter came by and discussed the results of the recent scan.

He said, "It looks good. It doesn't show any malignancy at this time."

My question was, "When can this man go fishing?" This question elicited big smiles from patient and doctor.

"Well, right now, today, if he feels like it!"

Dr. Erter was doing a magnificent job as Jim's oncologist. Dr.McKay had retired, even though we didn't think he needed to. I told him we'd be fine with his retirement if he would make sure he left us with another brilliant and capable oncologist, and it would have to be one who could put up with me! Jim and I sincerely appreciated his handing us over to Dr. Erter. We could not have been more pleased. I have thanked Dr. Erter many times for his care of Jim, and for putting up with me.

Jim was dismissed from the hospital, and Greg was also able to go home within the same week. Neither of them wasted any time before they went fishing. It was glorious, father and son on a fishing trip together! Sure wish Big Ron was able to be out there on the lake with them.

Our time between January and March were spent with a different focus. Jim was doing well, but his brother's health was steadily declining. Ronnie was aware that his time on this earth was short. He made the most of every moment with family and friends. He was able to manage getting his thoughts into words even when we had to play guessing games to find the right words. He knew exactly what he was trying to say. The exact words just didn't come out. It was endearing, and at times gave us all a jolt of Big Ron humor. He was able to tell everyone he loved them. He would say it each time they'd visit. Jim and I visited almost every day. One afternoon before we went to their home for our visit, Jim told me, "I don't think we need to go see him every day."

"We don't. He needs to see you. It has always been important to him to know you are ok." I told him. I was afraid a time might come when Ronnie would want to see Jim and wouldn't be able to communicate it.

Jim was able to handle Ronnie's illness and impending death in a calm manner. He and Ronnie had discussed this. Ronnie did not want Jim to die before him. Bottom line, case closed. Jim knew Ronnie was getting his way.

It was March 2012. Ronnie knew we were going to Houston for another check up. We went to see him the night before we left. He gave us the thumbs up sign and told us he loved us. We said we'd call him. We talked *about* him that trip more than we talked *with* him. When we called him to give him a travel update, his voice was sweet and his words loving. The tumors wouldn't let him calculate trip statistics any more.

The trip to Houston was made with good results. Dr. Fossella reported to us the cancer was in remission. That was wonderful news, but he wanted to see us again in May. I took a nosedive at that request. Suspecting the worst, I asked him why he wanted to see us in two months if we'd been coming there every three or four months. He told us he'd like to see Jim after he'd been off chemo for three months. He used the word remission. It was wonderful to be able to give Ronnie good news about Jim, even if it was the last time.

Ronnie died April 10, 2012.

There were times I didn't post anything about Jim's condition. It had been a tough four months. We needed a break from cancer and sickness. We needed to heal. We did, however, want our story to be told, the good, along with the not so good. Even if the story we must share is not the story we would have chosen. We didn't choose it, it chose us.

I knew the book would be forthcoming, but I would need to know when to end the story. I moved, exhaustedly, through days and weeks and months where I felt our story would help no one. Doubt and fear are tools the devil uses. He knows how to make me feel discouraged. He doesn't want God to be glorified. He is happier when he can cause a believer to give up. I was so close to feeding every page of the Houston trip notes to the shredder. The devil was on my shoulder. He was ridiculing me for even entertaining an idea of writing about our battles with cancer. One day I shared with one of my encouraging friends my temptation to go to the shredder. I received an email from her.

"What if Job's story hadn't been told?"

I began to write again with renewed energy. Thank God for the positive influences in life!

Our August 2012 Houston trip was another visit with good results. The cancer was still in remission. We were happy to have Mary go on the trip with us. She hadn't seen M.D. Anderson since the 1980's. We were excited for her to see the fabulous improvements they had made the last thirty years. It was good for her to go along and re-live some of the memories of Ronnie and our Houston trips. If he wasn't driving us, he traveled with us every mile of the way in his mind. Toward the end of his brief illness he was unable to determine any details of our trip, but we know he traveled with us in his heart. His own dear and special way of caring for us will be forever remembered. He loved Jim. He honored me often by letting me know how much he appreciated my taking care of his little brother. I appreciated those compliments. I thrived on them. There is no need for anyone to ever take his place He left a no vacancy sign.

CHAPTER 16

Our Guardian Angels May Need a Break

Our January 2013 M.D. Anderson visit put our emotions to the test. We had been actually looking forward to getting on the road, taking the four days away, driving to somewhere warm. We had spent months working on a detailed home improvement project. We worked day and night to get our part of the project to completion so we would not have to come home to bare floors and sawdust. We were tired. We were ready for a day without a paint roller or power saw. We were done with our part of the work. Kristy and her design team would handle the final phase. They were in charge of decorating. They would work while we were gone and we would come home to their fabulous transformation of our home.

The trip to Houston would serve the purpose for us to get away for a short time. We anticipated a good report. We had no reason to suspect anything but good. There had been no problems. He had been feeling well. He had a good appetite, an improved energy level, no weight loss, no fluid retention, no coughing or shortness of breath. He was doing well. Our trip to Houston was easy. We stopped when we needed to, but mostly we just drove.

Good company, good weather, good music, good snacks, the roar of a good engine, a new set of tires, prayers surrounding us. What else did we need? The drive was pleasant and effortless.

The next morning, we followed our normal format of tests and would plan on getting results the next morning. Life does not always go as planned, even as good as our plan might seem. When Dr. Fossella came in to give us the results, he told us an abnormality had been detected in one of the lymph nodes in the left side of Jim's neck. There were also two small spots in the top of his remaining lung. We would need to stay for a biopsy of the lymph node. It would be Friday before we could get results. This would stretch our visit out to ten days. We had no choice but to stay. We would make the best of it.

My mind raced between the worst and the best. The worst: The beast will kill him this time. It has won. It is the nature of the thymoma beast to return again and again. The best: Maybe just having had the chronic upper respiratory infection caused the lymph node to show an abnormality. Somewhere amidst the worst and best was the concern of the long standing effects of chemotherapy. I don't want cancer to kill him and I don't want chemotherapy to kill him. This really is not in my hands. I grew tired of my mind's wild goose chases that ended up nowhere. I just stopped with all the thinking. I was tired of wasting brain cells. We had sunshine and seventy-something degree weather. I had three books to read. There was no work for us to do. We could relax. We had a fresh pot of coffee. We were sitting beside a pool. We would make the best of it, but for now we had phone calls to make.

We might have been calm and relaxed in Texas, but we were hearing of violent wind and rainstorms in Tennessee. We were concerned about our family back home and were keeping a watch on the weather channel. Kristy and her children were enjoying working on the design project at our house. They were having fun working together and felt safe in our basement during the storm. In the early hours of the morning, Kristy's ex-husband phoned to see if they were okay, and to tell them that he had lost his house. A 150-year-old tree had been uprooted by the wind and tossed onto the roof of his house. The house was a total loss and would need to be rebuilt from the foundation up. The majority of the gigantic tree had landed on the roof over our grandson, Corbin's room. Everything on that half of the house from roof to the basement was demolished. If he'd been spending the night there at his dad's house, he could have been killed. No one could breathe when we thought of this. When pictures of the destruction were sent for us to see, we stared at them in disbelief. It was tragic, but lives were spared. In the days following, many good people rallied around them with offers of help and hope. Our family was once again being surrounded by the outpouring of God's love.

Meanwhile, another near tragedy was averted at our house. Kristy and her team were working on the design project at our house. They had worked late into the night. The faint smell of burning wires had begun that night and was becoming stronger. They couldn't find the source; however, it seemed to be confined to the basement. They weren't sure what to do. They felt if they left, the house would burn down. If they stayed, it would burn down with them in it. They decided to call the fire department. When the firemen arrived they found very hot and extremely dangerous wiring in a light fixture in the ceiling downstairs. It could have caused our house to burn to the ground had it not been discovered in time.

After learning of these two events, we felt God was handling more than the biopsy, and we needed to trust Him completely. He had spared us so much tragedy with these events at home. We knew He would carry us through the waiting for results from the biopsy of the lymph node.

Our days went by quietly and quickly. When time came to get the test results, we felt energized. We checked out of the hotel and took the shuttle to the hospital. We would either be up for more Houston or we'd be on the road toward home. We could deal with either, but we were well rested and hoping for a drive home. God was orchestrating this, not us.

The wait in the little room was getting to us. We sat there for almost three hours. Finally the doctor appeared and began to give us results. He told us he didn't have the written report yet, but would give us the oral report from pathology. He said if the written report was any different from the oral report, he would call us. Our heads were about to spin off. He told us it looked like the lymph node contained a malignancy.

"Then it's back." I said. "And it's in the lung too?"

"Yes. It looks that way. We can watch it for a while or we can begin chemotherapy. Call Dr. Erter when you get home. Come back here mid treatment."

This would be thymoma number four! The wind was knocked out of my sails. Yet neither of us was surprised. You kind of get that heads up feeling when you are told there needs to be a biopsy. You have a way of figuring your odds have dropped somewhere deep into the twilight zone. I felt myself circling a black hole again, grabbing for the edges, hoping not to fall back in again.

We were now free to go home. Take our bad news, find a cup of coffee, and hit the trail. We called our children. Well, Jim called them. I couldn't talk yet. They have figured out if Jim calls, then it is bad news. It takes me a while to restore my ability to speak without blubbering. I tried making one phone call. I called Mary and I blubbered. It was not good for either of us. So I stayed off the phone except to call my mother.

We decided to drive all night and get home before the snow fell in Nashville. I started driving after we got out of Houston. Jim napped and was happy when he woke up in Little Rock. We stopped for a late night breakfast at Waffle House. I sensed Jim was too sleepy to drive. I took over when we stopped for fuel. We got home at five thirty that Saturday morning. Just about an hour later the snow started. It was a beautiful contrast from the sunny days in the city full sick people. How peaceful and quiet and totally serene. Home felt good. I walked through every room of our house, seeing newly decorated rooms for the first time. I saw where the firemen had removed the bulbs. I could see and smell the burnt wires. I thanked God again and again for that part in His plan of caring for our family.

That afternoon our phone rang. It was Dr. Fossella. He called to give us the results of the written report.

"This report," he told us, "shows no malignancy in the lymph node."

He advised us to follow up with Dr. Erter but not to schedule chemo at this time. He said he would see us in Houston for a check up in three months. We'd be up for another trip to Houston by April. We thanked Dr. Fossella and we thanked God.

What do we make of this? God is in control. Not us. We can plan and orchestrate just about enough to make ourselves crazy, but no matter what, good or bad, God is in control. It is no good to worry or to fear. It just wastes energy.

There are questions for which we have no answers. We can't change some things. They are what they are. We can increase our faith in God by grabbing onto His hand and staying by His side through the scary times. We still have the two spots on the lung. They may be the thymoma monster again, and they may not be. God already knows the answer, and He is in charge of what happens next. Having faith that God is in control does not mean I will become complacent and forget about the spots on Jim's lung. We didn't get to this place after thirty one years of dealing with a deadly monster by just sitting waiting for someone to do something. We gather information, consider our options and take action. There were times of kicking and screaming and some major tire squalling, but we arrived here in one piece, just missing one lung. We are better and stronger and more committed than ever to win this battle against this monster. We know it is a big scary opponent, and it is sneaky and mean. But God is bigger and He knows just what to do with sneaky and mean.

We continue to pray, not just telling God what we want, but also thanking Him for what He has given us. We ask for strength for what comes next and enjoy every minute of life with those we love.

As this part of the story ends, and as I take a brief look over the ending, I realize it might seem to others that most of our story tells of an endless journey to M.D. Anderson Cancer Center and back. We made a total of eighteen trips from April 2009 to September 2013. In real life it has been much more than road trips. We have done the best when we've been faced with the worst. We struggle at times as anyone might. Our love for one another and our strength from God carries us through every single day. We are blessed to have a praying family and praying friends. Our prayer warriors are located all over this country and even abroad. We know they are there for us even when we don't ask them to pray. They just do. God hears and He answers those prayers. We have learned how to pray audaciously. We have learned to praise God and we have learned to accept His answers when they don't match up with our requests. We have learned to find peace and joy in the simple things of daily life. There are some hard lessons in life, but between those jolts of reality, there are beauties and blessings of life that can go unnoticed if we are hurrying through life with blinders on. I probably would never have learned patience had I not spent countless hours in hospital waiting rooms, waiting in surgical areas and waiting on physician's reports of test results. Together Jim and I have had some real bonus years though! As we think back to 1982, knowing that our future together looked bleak, we rejoice over the bonus time we were given. I am overwhelmed at God's goodness when I think about how He allowed Jim not only to live to see our children grow up, but He allowed us to see three grandchildren come into this world and become a precious part of our life.

We are entering into a time where Jim's body has taken some major hits from surgery, radiation and chemotherapy. We will move ever so cautiously if there is a need for further chemotherapy. Our oncologists are our allies through this battle. We know they care about us. That has been evident from the very first day we needed them in our lives. We have no fears. We keep hope as our number one emotion.

CHAPTER 17

Not Quite the End

Our story is not over. This feels like a good time to end the book. At this time Jim does not have cancer. He is not on chemo. We will continue to keep a watch on his health for as long as he is on this earth. I will continue to care for him as long as I have the presence of mind and the physical strength to do so.

We would like for our story to be a source of strength to those who need strength to go through their tough times. We want our story to give a message of hope in the midst of chaos. We want to make everyone aware of the heavy burden cancer puts on the shoulders of the family, and to remind all that we must let cancer's battle make us better, not bitter. We want others to know that it is worth it to have faith in God. We are too small to carry our burdens alone. We have not been alone. We have had so many acts of kindness come our way. It would be impossible to mention everything that was done for us. And it would be more than impossible to mention every person who has been a part of our journey.

We want to show others how perseverance and tenacity and trust in God helped to get us through each day. We want to give hope to others. We want others to be blessed by depending on God and learning to trust him. Trust does not come by giving up or giving in. It comes by keeping on even when you don't feel like it. That is what helped us one day at a time, sometimes one hour at a time, even minute by minute. It was difficult for me to decide to show my times of doubt and fear. I decided to share a portion of those emotions; because to show only the good parts, the days when the caregiver's job was a pleasure, would have been unbelievably fake.

By showing our daily activities through these times of trial, we hope it will be helpful to others who are dealing with cancer to know that other normal people made it through. We hope others will learn to find joy in the small pleasures of daily life. In sharing the many acts of kindness on our behalf, others can be aware of how they can assist those who are in the midst of crisis. We want to show how family, friends and faith work together as we all grab onto hope and hang on!

WHO WE ARE TODAY

I am an eternal neat-freak, a workaholic. Jim isn't. He likes his newspapers, magazines, mail and maybe a few pair of shoes scattered around the house. He likes for stuff to stay where he puts it. He hangs a shirt he might wear again on the bedpost. Closets are for shirts. I move the shirts when they get three deep. I suspect that when I go on a trip he celebrates by turning on every light in the house and hanging shirts on all four of the bedposts. I imagine he runs with scissors and leaves the garage door open so the clutter is visible to all. I bet the television is so loud that the neighbors don't need to turn theirs on. He cleans up the kitchen only one time while I am away, right before I come home. He starts washing dishes when I call to tell him I'm on my way home.

But, when I come home after a trip, there are clean sheets on the bed for me, a pot of coffee ready, my mail in a little stack, and a guy who loves me and missed me while I was gone. I couldn't ask for better.

We agree on all the important things. We try not to lose our sense of humor. When we disagree, we figure out a way to come together in a thought process that sometimes involves a little yelling. The children have always thought we argue funny because as heated as it may seem, someone says something to make the other laugh. I am usually the one who ends up laughing. He is the funny one. But, he is the one who has made the living, bought the houses, the cars, paid the bills and fed us for all these years. I will laugh at his lame jokes as long as he keeps them coming. He carries the laundry basket downstairs to the laundry area for me. He keeps my John Deere mower full of gasoline, and has even taught me to air up my own tires with the scary compressor in the garden shed. His having a cell phone while he's on the lake fishing helps me a lot. He always answers with,

"Yeah babe." and always knows the answer to whatever question I ask him.

We may be opposites—Jim, the country boy who grew up with little and finds more value in life than anyone I have ever known, and me, the always made-up city girl, with almost as much attitude as my little red mustang. I believe what we have here is the love story of a lifetime. I wouldn't trade what we share for the entire world.

Some Practical Helps When Visiting

Don't stay away because you want to remember them the way they were before they were sick. The visit is not about you. It is for them.

1. Call before you visit.
2. Wash your hands before and after. Don't visit if you have a cough or cold.
3. If the television is on, ask if you are interrupting an important show. Sometimes people have their television on for background noise, but it can be annoying if you are trying to have a conversation. They may turn it down or off, or you may have to talk around it. At our house we turn it off.
4. Follow the patient's lead in subject matter.
5. Listen as well as talk.
6. Plan to make the visit brief. The patient might insist you stay longer. Follow his lead.
7. Be positive and cheerful. Don't be the bearer of bad news. Don't bring up the subject of people who've died with cancer.
8. Don't ask personal questions.
9. Don't offer miracle cure ideas. If cancer could be cured by eating a certain food…really?

10. Don't wear cologne.
11. Turn off your cell phone (or at least silence it), and do not text.
12. Offer a prayer.

How to Save a Caregiver's Life

1. Tell them you appreciate the way they are caring for their loved one.
2. Listen more than you talk. Don't ask personal questions.
3. If they need to vent, let them. Then keep it to yourself.
4. Be positive. You might get teary-eyed, but save your breakdown for later.
5. Ask when would be a good time to bring a meal or dessert.
6. Ask what specific chore they'd like to see get done. If they can't or won't tell you, have one in mind.
7. Share good movies books, magazines or puzzles.
8. Ask what errands need to be done. Offer to sit with their loved one if they'd like.
9. Don't offer advice or give miracle cure ideas.
10. Even if you feel you've said it a hundred times, let them know you are thinking of and praying for them.
11. Always call first. The caregiver is taking care of the patient as well as the details of running the home. They might like to straighten up a bit or finish a chore before the visit.
12. Your visit should lift their spirits and encourage them.

Musings

1. Life is not fair. No one said it would be. Don't whine.
2. Everyone has problems. I can't change mine, but I can change how I react.
3. Happiness is something we choose.
4. Tears are soul cleansers. Prayer is a better soul cleanser.
5. Love the person you see in the mirror. God does.
6. It is okay to be mad at God. It is not okay to *stay* mad at God.
7. Tell God you are mad. He knows it. Pray it out.
8. Don't take advice from someone you wouldn't want to exchange places with.
9. A positive attitude benefits you more than a negative one.
10. In life, we will experience negative emotions. Identify each one; handle one at a time. Don't let them stack up on top of each other.
11. Sadness does not have to stay.
12. Home sickness won't kill you. It makes you appreciate home when you are there.
13. Don't deny others the joy of helping you. Pass it on.
14. Think about what you want to have happen. Practice positive expectancy.

15. Reaching out to others helps you refill your pitcher but it also empties it. Be sure you get refills often. You cannot pour out of an empty pitcher.
16. It is okay to take time for yourself. Eat. Exercise. Read. Sleep.
17. Talking *with* someone is different that talking *to* someone. Do both.
18. You don't always have to have your way. Listen to others. Hear with your heart.
19. God made us all unique and precious. See others that way.
20. The only thing you'll get from looking back is a sore neck.
21. Break away from the mold that others put you in. Let God mold you instead.
22. Don't cast your pearls before the swine. It is difficult to get mud out of good jewelry.
23. Cry if you need to. You'll feel better after your nose returns to its regular color.
24. Let people know you love them.
25. Practice random acts of kindness.
26. Praise God more than you petition Him.
27. Go one whole day without saying "I want".
28. Enter a room and let your body language say: "Oh there you are" instead of "Oh look, here I am!"
29. Don't seek the chief seat in the room. When you are in the chief seat, don't turn around and look behind you. It makes you look simple.
30. Taking a walk improves every part of your life.
31. Ask an older person anything about their life and watch them light up. Listen without interrupting.

32. Eat popcorn.

33. Go barefooted in the rain.

34. Don't be afraid to laugh at yourself.

35. Treat children as the delicate creatures they are. Look into their eyes.

36. Treat elderly people as the delicate creatures they are. See the child in them.

37. Be happy about your age. Each year is precious.

38. Don't be a bully and don't be hateful.

39. Send a note thanking a veteran for fighting for your freedom, and winning.

40. Cook someone's favorite food and take it to them.

41. If someone compliments you on something you have and you feel like parting with it, give it to them. I enjoy the things I've given away much more than the ones I've kept.

42. Never lose your sense of humor.

43. Sing. Even if you don't know how.

44. Learn a new word every day. Never forget the meaning of some of the most important ones: love, peace, joy, contentment, grace.

45. Go to bed early sometimes.

46. Don't try to fix everybody.

47. Write the story of your life for your grandchildren. Begin it with "Once upon a time..."

48. Tell your spouse that, next to God, you love him/her more than anything in this world.

49. Hug your parents and let them know you love them.

50. Send a note to a person who is sick. Address it to both the patient and spouse. Both of them are dealing with the illness.

Gratitude

In my lifetime, many people have influenced me positively. I owe these people immeasurably more than I have to give.

My parents, Floyd and Jean Fetzer, were the first ones to instill in me that I was tough enough, smart enough, and talented enough to get the job done and look good doing it. Because of them I have never backed away from a challenge, even those that seemed unrealistic and insurmountable. I have been the best *me* I could be.

Even though my sister, Debby and my brother, David had to put up with me and my "oldest child syndrome" attitude for so many years, we've actually grown to like each other. Thanks for your patience with me.

My Aunt Bessie, who was an English teacher and a writer, encouraged my writing. I have always loved books, reading and writing. I will write for the rest of my life, and I owe to her the spark that ignited my desire. It was thrilling to read her book "Mountains and Valleys", The Life and Times of Bessie Fetzer Williams." It was published about 1993.

I couldn't have our story published until our children were grown. Their having lived through this as children was enough; they didn't need to relive it in a book. Greg and Kristy, if this life experience warped you in any way, maybe you will find some healing in these pages. We all made it through just fine. I'm proud of who you've become. Even after all this, we still couldn't have asked for a better life.

My granddaughters, Morgan and Mallory, who share with me a knack for words and possess the computer skills I lack, deserve thanks as well. This would be scribed on parchment if not for those two. My grandson and personal comedian, Corbin, has a way of easing life's stresses with his brilliant wit. Thanks for keeping us laughing.

My husband, Jim personally experienced cancer's devastating blow to his body. He endured it as the patient. He was the one who had to go through surgery, radiation and several courses of chemotherapy. He lives each day with no bitterness, negativity or regret. He is a good man. He goes about life in a humble way. I regret he had to endure cancer for us to have a story to be told.

Finally, this venture might have been another thirty one years in the making if not for the encouragement of my friends, family, and blog readers. Special thanks to Anne M. Clark and Michael C. Raymond. Your support means more to me than I can say.

CPSIA information can be obtained at www.ICGtesting.com
Printed in the USA
LVOW13s0350181013

357421LV00002B/4/P